SUICIDE

UNMASKED

Exploring the missing key to understanding suicide

DR. BILL SHADE

SUICIDE UNMASKED

By: Dr. Bill Shade

ISBN-13:978-1544191041

ISBN-10:1544191049

Printed in the United States of America

Copyright © 2017 by Dr. Bill Shade

All rights reserved solely by the author. No part of this book may be reproduced in any form without the written permission of the author.

Unless otherwise indicated, Bible quotations are taken from the (KJV) King James Version of the Bible

Other versions referenced are:
(CEV) Contemporary English Version
(ISV) International Standard Version
(ASV) American Standard Version

Cover by Heather Wilson

Visit our website at: BillShade.org

DEDICATION

*To all those whose hearts have broken
for a loved one who chose to leave before
their time –
and to those too, who have wrestled
with the temptation to do so.*

CONTENTS:

Foreword IX

Introduction 1

Chapter 1: The Extent of the Problem 3

Chapter 2: Reasons Behind The Act 7

Chapter 3: Circumstances 23

Chapter 4: The Mind – How We Think 31

Chapter 5: The Enigma of Suicide 35

Chapter 6: The Bible Record 45

Chapter 7: There Is a Strategy 57

Chapter 8: Suicide Unmasked 61

Chapter 9: The Warning Signs 75

Chapter 10: My Perspective 83

Chapter 11: You and God 89

Chapter 12: Standing Your Ground 95

Chapter 13: Resisting the Enemy 101

Chapter 14: Faithful Sayings 109

Footnotes I

FOREWORD

Pastors expect to deal with difficult situations on a somewhat regular basis, but the situation I faced that day was more than difficult. Besides, I was young having been a pastor for only about five years. During that time I had seen God use us to have an extensive ministry through both the local church, my radio broadcast (which had become very popular in the mountain region), and our mission outreach to the public high schools where I regularly visited twenty-seven schools in seven counties.

As a result of these various ministries, I had become well known throughout the area and was either loved or hated, depending usually on the perspective of the individual toward my straightforward approach to Scripture and its application. As a result, I was called upon frequently to do the weekly devotional on the radio, when some other pastor decided he was too busy to take the time, or to conduct a funeral for someone who was without a church home.

So when our local undertaker called and asked me to come to the funeral home, it wasn't something terribly unusual. Nevertheless, the tone of Durward's voice had left me with a strange feeling of apprehension.

It was a cold winter day and it seemed unusually cold as I drove into the parking lot and got out of my car. By now, the apprehension had grown to serious concern and I wondered what I was about to encounter.

Durward met me at door and soberly welcomed me in with, "Thanks for coming preacher." As we walked into the morgue, he said, "I have a body I need to have identified. I know who it is, but I have to have corroboration – I didn't want to call his wife to do that."

With that he led me to a morgue table where I saw the sheeted form of a body, apparently in a semi-sitting position. "The body was frozen when we found him," Durward offered, "I have it propped up in this position until it thaws." And with that he pulled the sheet down to reveal the upper torso of the man on the table.

What I saw shocked me then, and was so vivid that now, many decades later, I can still see it as if it were yesterday. There on the table, propped up in a sitting position, was the body of a man I knew well. I looked into the sightless eyes of one who a few short months before had been a deacon and a close dear friend. Just above his heart was a puncture wound from a bullet. I confirmed Durward's identification and then asked, "Durward, what happened?"

I knew the man I was looking at was a state trooper. He was well respected and known for his honesty and integrity. I wondered if he had been in some kind of gun battle, or if someone with a grudge had killed him. "Suicide," Durward said bluntly. My mind raced.

I thought back to shortly after I had come to the community. I remembered his wife and young children. I remembered that day years before when I was just driving home and realized there was a fire truck ahead of me going up the main hollow in our little community. In a moment, it stopped in front of Eddie's (fictitious name) home.

The home was ablaze and I stopped to help. The volunteer fire crew asked me to drag a hose as they turned on the pumps to try to control the fire. It was quickly evident that the main task would be to keep the fire from spreading to the homes on either side, for this house was clearly beyond saving.

After the excitement, I learned that their son, the youngest of the children, had found a pack of matches and was entertaining himself by lighting them in the closet. Thankfully, all of the children and their mother got out without injury. But my next question was where would they now live – they had lost everything?

Ours was a mining community and there just weren't too many choices. When we first came to the community Ruby and I had stayed in a small apartment on the first floor of the Union Hall, but it was hardly adequate for two people, much less a whole family and the only toilet available was one that belonged to the restaurant across the hallway.

After Ruby and I had lived there for awhile, we asked the deacons to allow us take one of the classrooms in the church basement and live there until we got our home. It was small, but there was a full kitchen and toilets and we had lived there for a number of months in comparative comfort.

So, we immediately placed the family there at no charge until they could find something else. That had been the beginning of a wonderful relationship with the family and soon all but Daddy were coming to church.

My mind then jumped to that day when that same man had stopped me on the main street of our nearest town. We were planning as a church to have a tent crusade and he knew we needed money so he kindly pressed a bill into my hand for the project. I thanked him, but taking his hand and looking straight into his eyes I asked, "Eddie, do you know Jesus as your Savior? Are you a Christian?"

He answered that he was not and I gently returned the bill. "God doesn't want what you have," I told him, "God wants you." He later told me it was the first time a preacher had ever turned down money he had offered, but it shook him sufficiently that he attended that crusade and one night accepted Christ as his personal Savior.

All of that and more raced through my mind as I stood there in the morgue stunned. Why? Why, would he do this? What could possibly drive a fine Christian and a respected law officer to take his own life? How could I tell his wife and children? What would they do now? How could they even live? I was to find out in the days that followed.

INTRODUCTION

I hate suicide! Why would anyone write a book on such a distasteful subject? Who would want to read it? Why delve into something so ugly and repulsive?

I have had the unfortunate experience of having to deal with a number of people within my sphere of friends and acquaintances who have chosen to take their own lives. As a result, I have walked through that labyrinth of emotional responses that always accompanies such events.

The cycle begins with shock and the sheer horror of the event itself. Suicides are never pretty and often they are scenes that are so terrible we can never completely get them out of our memories.

Then there follows a deep sense of sadness and grief. We remember the life and often the pleasant times we enjoyed with the now deceased. We hear their voice and see their face, meet them in our dreams – often for years to come.

All our remembering begins to raise questions. What part did I have in this tragedy? What could I have done to prevent it? Did I do, or say anything that might have triggered it or even contributed to what happened here? Real or imagined guilt sets in and the emotional pain increases.

Then there follows anger. We contemplate the folly of the act – the utter thoughtlessness toward those who loved or cared. Did they ever think of the effect their self-centered act would have upon others. What about the influence of what they have done upon those who looked up to them – influence to act in the same way – and believe me, every study shows that one act of suicide is a powerful factor in multiple suicides and so-called suicide clusters.

Finally, when the anger begins to be assuaged, rational thought takes over and we rightfully ask, "Why did this happen?" "What were the factors that led to this?" And most importantly, "Is there a common thread that runs through events like this?" "Is there a 'missing Key' to understanding and confronting suicide?"

After years of observation and with the examination of Scripture itself, I am convinced that there is, and that if we can confront that one common factor, we can do much toward defeating this robber of potentially productive and fruitful lives. Exploring the missing key to understanding suicide is the focus of this book.

Chapter One

THE EXTENT OF THE PROBLEM

Statistics are always changing and that means that before they are in print they are already obsolete. Nevertheless, it would be irresponsible to tackle a subject like this without some reference to its widespread nature.

I have not even attempted to cull statistics on a worldwide basis, but have simply focused on this country. However, on a country by country basis, the United States ranks 43rd in suicides per capita, and that should give us some idea what this may look like on a global scale.

The World Health Organization (WHO), estimated that in the year 2000 approximately 1,000,000 (that's one million), people would die from suicide. A global mortality rate of 16 per 100,000 – <u>one death by suicide every 40 seconds</u>.[1]

In that same year (2000), WHO further reported that, in the past 45 years, suicide rates had increased by 60% worldwide. Suicide had become one of the three leading causes of death among those aged 15-44 (both sexes), and beyond the number of those who actually commit suicide, suicide attempts are up to 20 times more frequent than completed suicides.[2]

SUICIDE AMONG YOUTH
Traditionally, suicide rates have been highest among elderly males. However, rates among young people have

been increasing to such an extent that the young are now the group at highest risk in a third of all countries.

While writing this book, I recently visited a patient in a specialized therapy hospital in central Georgia. While there I was told, "of the 42 beds in this facility, 22 of them are occupied by young people going through extreme depression or who are suicidal."

The World Health Organization (WHO), states that, "Mental disorders (particularly depression and substance abuse) are associated with more than 90% of all cases of suicide." Please note that "mental disorders" is a very broad designation and one which I want to examine much more closely as we move forward.

WHO concludes that, "suicide results from many complex socio-cultural factors and is more likely to occur during periods of socioeconomic, family and individual crisis (e.g. loss of a loved one, employment, honor)."[3] And let's not forget to mention copycat suicides – the suicide of someone else, even someone unknown to the original person committing suicide.

At the turn of the century, the Centers for Disease Control (CDC) in the US, were reporting that: "More people die from suicide than from homicide." The CDC then reported that there were 1.5 times as many suicides as homicides. Back then, suicide was the eighth leading cause of death for all Americans, and the third leading cause of death for young people aged 15-24.

However, as I stated at the beginning, things are changing so rapidly that even that report is now out of date and the Jason Foundation, in its *Youth Suicide Statistics - Parent Resource Program*, reports that Suicide is now the SECOND leading cause of death for college-age youth and those ages 12-18. According to the report, "More teenagers and young adults die from suicide than from cancer, heart disease, AIDS, birth defects, stroke, pneumonia, influenza, and chronic lung disease, combined."[4]

And not only have the figures for youth suicides changed, but according to NBC news, overall rates of suicide have soared 24 percent in the U.S. since the turn of the century. [5]

Most disquieting is the pattern of "suicide clusters" that seem to be in the news on an almost daily basis. During the last 13 months, there have been nine deaths in one school district, between two schools located only a mile apart. And in a nearby city, there were five student suicides last month. And these recent deaths follow 29 student suicides that occurred in the same area between 2013 and 2015.

SUICIDE AND THE MILITARY
Another distressing phenomena is the acceleration of suicides among the military community. NBC reported that, "Historically, suicide rates in the Army have been half that of the nation – being in the Army was protective against suicide."[6] That has now changed.

In 2012 military suicides across the four branches of service hit a record 349 men and women who took their own lives. Although that has now moderated slightly (down to 269 in 2014), it is obvious we are facing a major crisis among a societal group that had traditionally had one of the lowest numbers of suicides.

The VA (Veterans Administration) now reports that 20 military, or former military, die each day from self-inflicted causes.[7] It is hard to comprehend, but that is twenty a day.

Something has changed – what is it? Why is suicide so prevalent among our military? Why is it now the second leading cause of death among Air Force personnel?

We need to find the answers, and so with this brief glimpse at some very disquieting statistics, I think we can confidently say that we have a clear and present danger – a crisis that must be addressed.

Let's again ask the question, "Why does it happen and what can be done to stop the carnage?"

Chapter Two

REASONS BEHIND THE ACT

For many years I traveled to various high schools and lectured on current topics. The most popular of all of those lectures and the one most requested – sometimes for a second and even a third year in a row, was a lecture I did on suicide.

One outgrowth of that was that often teens would come to me, after the assembly program and want to talk about their personal situation. There were several that particularly stand out as memorable and help illustrate some of the apparent causes for suicide.

1. Feelings of Rejection
It was not uncommon when I would talk about suicide in a school venue to get several notes handed to me by students. These were obviously cries for help and they were frequently heartbreaking and sometimes down right alarming.

Many of them began something like this one which was handed to me by a young girl who barely raised her head to look at me as she walked by. It said: "I'm so timid I can't talk so I've written you this note . . . I feel so worthless . . . everything I try to do turns out wrong . . . I'm just taking up space . . ."

Although both heartbreaking and alarming, that note was not unusual. It spoke the feelings of many teens whom I counseled with during those days and many who have attempted suicide. The most recent note left at a teen suicide said, "I think everyone would be better off without me."

In his classic book *The Ins and Outs of Rejection*, Charles Solomon puts his finger on the central dynamic in play in this kind of a suicide when he writes, Suicide is "the ultimate in self-rejection and the epitome of self-centeredness."[8]

Notice the apparent contradiction in that statement. We do not think of self-rejection and self-centeredness as parallel emotions, but Solomon clearly shows that they are. The connecting link is the word **self**.

Feelings of worthlessness and rejection may come from any number of factors, but they are directly related to a total focus on **self**. Whenever there is a focus on **self**, it leads inevitably, either to delusions of grandeur, or to despair or self-rejection.

Focus on **self** is a sure sign of deep problems, and it is frequently found in teens who are struggling though the issues of hormonal change and approaching or going through puberty. Rejection or perceived rejection by peers at this stage can push self-rejection over the edge. And that leads us to a second reason for suicide.

2. Feelings of Guilt
Another strong emotion which often accompanies suicide is the feeling of guilt. Modern psychiatry would attempt to deal with guilt as something to be ignored or repressed, but as Dr. Clyde Narramore once observed, "People feel guilty because they are guilty."[9]

I remember meeting K. at one of the schools where I lectured. This young lady was an exceptional student and a committed Christian who had been chosen to go as an exchange student to South America.

She told me how she had been placed in a secular environment with a family who were non-Christians. At first she had determined to be a good testimony to them and had located a small evangelical church not far from her host family's home where she could attend.

As is often characteristic in a strongly Catholic country, the handful of believers that met there, met in a small storefront rather than a formal church building. K's attendance there greatly embarrassed the host family who felt themselves socially above the people who gathered there.

Soon the family began to scoff at K. for her religious affiliations and her convictions. Gradually the pressure became more than she was willing to bear. She quit going to the services, then quit praying, then quit reading the Scripture.

One night at a teenage dance, she violated her conscience and was so overcome by guilt that she attempted to get her hands on a gun she knew to be kept in the house. Once the host family became aware of what was happening, they took precautions by locking the gun away.

Next, K. tried to electrocute herself in the shower and had to be rushed to the hospital. Finally, she tried an overdose of drugs. At that, she was sent home and that is where I met her.

K. had finally worked through her trauma and realized that her guilty conscience was the root of her desperate behavior. She had confessed her sin and was free to talk with me about her previous problems.

While we are focusing on the part guilt can play in suicidal thoughts and attempts, it must be remembered that these various causes or forces at work do not necessarily act alone. Actually, they often act upon a person in tandem – guilt leads to self rejection and other negative emotions which interplay to bring about feelings of despair.

3. Drug Abuse

One of the major reasons for the increase in suicide among teens (and adults), has been the increase of drug usage beginning in the run-away 1960's, continuing and exploding at the present time.

While the "drugs of choice" have changed, running the gamut from the use of marijuana and LSD to crack cocaine and the more sophisticated methamphetamines (and more recently even prescription drugs), the incidence of usage among teens has only increased.

What role do drugs play in the increase in suicide? Drugs were listed as a significant factor in 75% of the suicides which occurred in the Boston "cluster" where in 1997, six teens committed suicide, while 70 were hospitalized in suicide attempts."[10]

In 1986 Dexter Gardner, a teen in Texas, committed suicide after making a tape recording for his parents to listen to. Some of what he said may be instructive in trying to understand the part drugs can play in suicide, so I am including part of the actual text from the recording. I often used the recording when doing assemblies on the subject. Gardner said:

> *This may come as a shock to you mom, but your little boy is a drug addict. It's really bad Mom. I didn't think it was when I first got into it, but my*

mind is blown . . . I don't know what's right and what's wrong anymore, I don't know what's real and what isn't real.

Ah, . . . the reason I'm doing this . . . well, the real reason is I don't know . . . So, all I can say is, I'm not going to make any sentimental speeches if you know what I mean, so I'll just close with a blank statement, maybe a kind of idiotic statement, but a lot of things are crazy these days . . . so I'll just close by saying; This is Dexter Gardner speaking, . . . I'm signing off." (Then a gun shot is heard). [11]

One statement above may be worth special note. Gardner said, "I'm signing off." In radio-speak terminology he was saying that the program was ended, the set was off.

But when lecturing, I have often noted that Scripture clearly reveals that death does not end our existence – it only closes one door, to open another. Gardner may have thought that he was turning off the set but, in fact, he only changed the channel, and the new program he woke up to may have been much less to his liking than the one he had tried to escape. Eternity is real and suicide does not end anything but your opportunity to change your eternal destination.

4. Influence of Music / Books / TV / Films

Along with the loss of reality brought on through the use of drugs can be the very similar effect of the hypnotic power of music, films and other media.

Heavy metal themes of death, which often glorify suicide, create strong impressions which never completely go away. This is especially true when young minds are repeatedly and powerfully exposed to such themes.

The very names of certain popular music groups strongly suggest themes of death and violence. Add to this, popular books like Dereck Humphry's *Final Exit*, which is a veritable "how to" manual for suicide, and it is no wonder that suicide records show clear and unmistakable connections between these influences and the increasing rate of suicide in our time.

The National Federation of Decency reported the following statistics in an article entitled, *Does TV Corrupt Children:*

> To date, 28 people have killed themselves playing Russian Roulette after watching the movie THE DEERHUNTER on television.
>
> Seventeen-year-old Cathy Ann Petruso and (a few weeks later), her ex-boyfriend hanged themselves just like a character did in AN OFFICER AND A GENTLEMAN following the breakup of his romance. Petruso and her boyfriend had seen the movie together several times.
>
> A fourteen-year-old boy saw rock music star Alice Cooper do a mock-hanging on TV and tried the stunt himself—he succeeded in hanging himself. [12]
>
> Another teen relates how one night after swim practice, she was taking a bath and listening to a moody Alicia Keys song on a CD her mom had bought her. She'd taken a bottle of Advil from a cabinet downstairs and as she listened to the music, she swallowed all the pills. Thankfully, a parent found the empty bottle and her life was spared.

There are recorded cases of attempted suicide after films like *Pandora, Suicide Squad* and *Twilight.* Films have the power to strongly influence the emotions and actions of people, especially young people and the memories of them sometimes last a lifetime.

The Netflix series **13 Reasons Why** deals frankly with a teenage girl's suicide, including a tough-to-watch 3-minute scene of the suicide itself. A study published in the *Journal of American Medicine* wants Netflix to pull the show. The study found that online searches about suicide increased by 19% over a 19-day span, "reflecting 1.5 million more searches than expected."

Some additional facts:
- "Suicide hotline number" calls were up 21%. for example.
- "How to commit suicide" searches rose 26%.
- "Commit suicide" rose 18%.
- "How to kill yourself" rose 9.

John Ayers of San Diego State University, speaking on CNN said, "Our worst fears (about the effects of the show) were confirmed, . . . thousands of people are searching online about ways to kill themselves." He called for Netflix to pull the show and stop filming season 2. 13

Child psychiatrists say their patients are bringing up the show. The *Washington Post* reports that at Cincinnati Children's Hospital a 12-year-old girl told her psychiatrist, "I saw that show and it really convinced me that suicide was a normal thing to do." The psychiatrist said. "I've never heard that. In 30 years, I've never heard a child say this thing made me think suicide is normal. That really got my attention." 14

I received the following in a letter from a teen where I had spoken at the school assembly about suicide.

"Alberta was drinking heavily and listening to her favorite groups – Slayer, Anthrax, AC/DC, Iron Maiden, Alice Cooper, Quiet Riot, you name it – Alberta listened to them all. That night while she was drunk, she took a razor blade and carved every single band and group she listened to into her body.

Her body was covered from head to toe and she died from too much loss of blood. At her funeral, they couldn't even keep the casket opened because the words cut into her body were so bad."

Remember, the producers of the current genre of music, films and other media have no conscience about the impact they have to distort reality and conjure up fear and confusion. Their only concern is the bottom line and the more horror they can pack into the product, the more tantalizing it is to young minds.

5. The Result of Failure or Personal Loss

There can be no doubt that suicide frequently comes on the heels of great personal loss or tragedy. In eastern lands, it has long been a tradition to take one's life when faced with failure of any kind. In certain cultures, "loss of face" or disgrace, resulting from personal failure, actually obligates one to commit suicide.

Suicide has been the traditional way for Japanese to handle any personal failure, from loss of wealth, to loss of love or even the loss of a sporting contest. Obviously, suicide is not an acceptable response in a Christian Ethical System, and we will discuss that more thoroughly later. But suicide because of failure or perceived failure has become more common among high school students in some of the more competitive schools in this country.

In 2014, Gunn High School in Silicon Valley, California, was ranked by *U.S. News & World Report* as one of the nation's top five STEM schools. Every year, about 20 of its seniors get into Stanford, which is just two miles away, and a quarter are offered spots at University of California schools, which are notoriously competitive. [15]

But despite the apparent and outward success, this Silicon Valley School is in trouble. In fact, Palo Alto High, another Silicon Valley school is also in trouble. The 10-year suicide rate for Gunn and Palo Alto High is between four and five times the national average.

When research was conducted to learn why the best and most affluent schools in the country should have the distinction of also being the schools most prone to student suicide, researchers found that parents and faculty had "given their kids the idea that they had to perform, that love or recognition had to be earned with A's and Advanced Placement tests and trophies."[16]

After leaving Stanford, Julie Lythcott-Haims wrote a book, called *How to Raise an Adult: Break Free of the Overparenting Trap and Prepare Your Kid for Success*. In it, she detailed the growing mental-health crisis at colleges, and described the brilliant, accomplished students who "would sit on my couch holding their fragile, brittle parts together, resigned to the fact that this outwardly successful situation was their miserable life."[17] The kids had internalized their parents' priorities and didn't know how to break free.

Bill Blackburn in his classic book on Suicide makes this poignant observation, "Suicide is a permanent solution to a temporary problem."[18] In fact, suicide is not a solution at all. Suicide does not solve any problem; it rather seeks to run from the problem only to face another.

6. Fear of the Future
As has already been observed, reasons for suicide are often complex and cannot be reduced to a single issue. However, one very strong influence in the phenomena of suicide is the element of fear.

Alongside loss (especially of wealth or of health) comes the uncertainty of being able to cope with the future. That uncertainty, if not met with faith, will inevitably lead to fear. This comes from a number of related problems ranging from an obsession with the evening news, to various real or imagined health problems, even financial fears -- remember the Wall Street crash that started the Great Depression?

The current demand for the legal right for doctor assisted suicide grows largely out of the motivation of a fear of the future. Sometimes it is simply a fear of pain, as in the advanced stages of cancer and other diseases. The movement toward legalized euthanasia is related to this as well and continues to dominate the media.

SOUNDING BOARD of the "New England Journal of Medicine" published an article entitled, "Rational Suicide and the Right to Die." It was written by a group of psychiatrists who worked with suicidal people and helped them make adjustments so that suicide no longer seemed necessary.

They also conducted "psychological autopsies" of all suicides in Monroe County in New York. Their findings are significant:

"Of 85 suicides in a study presented to the American Psychological Association (APA), only one victim had a diagnosed terminal illness, yet each was driven to self destruct." [19]

The last stage of fear is a feeling of despair and doom and finally suicide.

For the believer, please notice how the very things which lead to suicide prove how wrong it is. Scripture tells us, *God hath not given us the spirit of fear; but of power, and of love, and of a sound mind* (2 Timothy 1:7).

7. Bullying

In recent years, a series of bullying-related suicides in the US and across the globe have drawn attention to the connection between bullying and suicide. Bullying is typically defined as the ongoing physical or emotional victimization of a person by another person or group of people.

Though many adults still see bullying as "just part of being a kid," it is a serious problem that leads to many negative effects for victims, including suicide. There is also a clear, demonstrable link between acting the part of a bully and committing suicide.

Keep in mind that for every suicide among young people, there are at least 100 suicide attempts. Over 14 percent of high school students say they have considered suicide, and almost 7 percent have attempted it. [20]

Now here is the statistic that is most pertinent to this discussion. Bully victims are between 2 to 9 times more likely to consider suicide than non-victims, according to studies by Yale University. [21]

According to statistics reported by ABC News, nearly 30 percent of students in public schools are either bullies or victims of bullying, and 160,000 kids stay home from school every day because of fear of bullying. [22]

Furthermore, bullying itself has changed. What used to be a war of words and insults (which can be hurtful enough), and at worse a fist fight on the playground, has degenerated, with the general moral tenor of the day, to extremely vicious behavior intended to totally destroy the victim.

A few years ago you would hear youngsters call, "sticks and stones may break my bones, but names can never hurt me." Of course, the fact is, names did hurt, even then.

But this is a new era, and words, accusations, false rumors, and abuse beyond anything former generations have known, is now common, even among adults. It is now known that bullying, and especially chronic bullying, has long-term effects on suicide risk and can persist into adulthood.[23]

8. Cyberbullying

With the advent of social media, Bully-related suicide is no longer confined to physical or verbal abuse on the playground (or classroom), but now we have bullying through social media called, Cyberbullying, meant to harass and cause emotional harm to their victims. And Cyberbullying has become epidemic. If that statement sounds extreme, just google the subject and you will find pages of evidence that it is not an exaggeration.

Cyberbullying takes many vicious forms including *sexting* (suggesting or demanding the person have sex with the sender), or circulating suggestive or nude photos or ugly messages about a person. According to the study, 10 to 14-year old girls are at the highest risk for suicide as a result of this kind of bullying.

And the perpetrators may not just be vicious teens. Parents, -- Yes, I said parents, jealous of another child's grades, looks, family social status or most anything else, have been known to pose as another teen and set up an elaborate online scheme to destroy the victim through social media.

A young girl posted the following on Change.org:

"My name is Elizabeth. A couple of years ago, when I was a junior in high school, I tried to commit suicide. While still recovering, I started receiving harassing messages on social media telling me I should try again to take my life. I'm lucky to have survived, and am now working to heal and use my experience to help others." [24]

9. Sexual Disorientation

Tragically, there is a new category of "at risk" persons especially among youth and teens. The situation is aided by the now politically correct attitude which seeks to affirm and normalize gender and sexual dysphoria, rather than identifying it as a pathology and seeking to treat it.

As a result, these persons have joined the LGBTQ community and have thus gained the double jeopardy of personal feelings of guilt and the rejection (if only implicit), of many of their peers.

The whole struggle for acceptance and the corresponding feelings of alienation often present in youth, are then exacerbated to the extreme when accompanied by gender dysphoria (or gender confusion).

The statistics speak for themselves: while "4.6 percent of the overall U.S. population has self-reported a suicide attempt, the situation among so-called 'transgender' youth is so serious that almost 50% have seriously thought about suicide, and more than 30% of LGBTQ youth report at least one suicide attempt within the last year." [25]

Frankly, this is more than tragic, and points to the fact that gender dysphoria is accompanied by all kinds of feelings of identity confusion, shame, guilt, and self-rejection.

The current "Politically Correct" (PC), approach is to affirm feelings of a cross-gender identity and often confirm them with everything from hormonal therapy to surgical alteration.

Unfortunately, this is often a very disastrous approach in the long term, because trying to normalize and enforce gender dysphoria is, according to the American College of Pediatricians, (and the latest report from John Hopkins University), . . . "both dangerous and unethical."[26]

10. To Make a Dramatic Statement
When self-styled prophet, Jim Jones, urged his deluded followers to drink from vats of Kool-aid laced with cyanide, he told them that what they were doing was, "an act of revolutionary suicide protesting the conditions of an inhumane world."[27] Their suicide was intended to make a powerful statement.

Actually, suicide is always meant to make a statement. It is, by its very nature, an act of rebellion.

The motivation to suicide, like all other forms of sinful behavior, has its origin in our own sinful nature, which Satan then acts upon to inflame to sinful action. But not all motivation is the same.

In my experience with those who have either attempted suicide, or strongly considered it, there were always one of several motives behind the contemplated action.

We have already discussed at some length the motivation of **despair** (if indeed despair can be called a motivation). It seems to be the great de-motivator, but in reality, it can become the driving force behind the desire and act of suicide.

Despair comes from a dissatisfaction with life and a belief that whatever situation it is that I hate, will never change. Basically, despair is a loss of hope.

There is a very insightful line in the classic story of Anne of Green Gables. Anne, in one of her typical, over-dramatic moments asks Marilla, "Haven't you ever been in despair?" To which Marilla replies, "No. To despair is to deny God." Precisely!

Another prime motivator for suicide is **anger** and a desire for revenge. The suicidal person would like to take out that anger on the person who has caused his (or her) misery, but since that is not possible, he turns the anger upon himself and seeks to get to the other person through harming himself. Statements such as, "you'll be sorry when . . ." demonstrate that the force behind the action is selfish anger and rage.

Along with anger is a desire for a kind of **revenge.** One of the questions we need to ask a person contemplating suicide is, "If you do what you are planning to do, who do you think would find your body?"

A follow up question would be, "How do you think your suicide will make that person feel?" The answers to those two questions will reveal who the person's anger is aimed at and what revenge they are seeking by causing sorrow and grief for the other person.

In an article on suicide from Compton's Encyclopedia we find this astute observation:

> "The individual, in seemingly hopeless conflict with the world, decides to end his or her existence in what amounts to a final temper tantrum against a society that can no longer be tolerated. In so doing, the person symbolically obtains a final revenge on everything and

everyone that has caused these feelings of depression."[28]

In the final analysis, suicide is an act of rebellion toward God. It is the person's way of telling God that he (or she) is angry at God for whatever it is in life that the person thinks is unfair. After all, if God is really God, then He has the final say in my circumstances so if I don't like them I can make a "revolutionary protest against Him." If what I have just said is true, then suicide is really a spiritual matter and we fail if we do not recognize that fact.

In the next two sections, we want to expand on two additional reasons or factors that play into the desire to commit suicide. After that, we will place the spiritual dimensions of suicide under the spot-light and begin to "Unmask Suicide."

Chapter Three

OTHER FACTORS:
CIRCUMSTANCES

In a discussion of suicide, one of the things which must be observed is the circumstances that surrounded, or lead up to the tragic decision to take one's life. I have already alluded to this in several of the cases I have personally dealt with and the same thing is evident in others which I have learned of.

I opened this book with the story of Eddie's suicide and asked myself the obvious, "What would cause a respected officer of the law, a former deacon, and a loving father to put a gun to his heart and pull the trigger?" As the weeks after the shooting passed by, some of the answers began to emerge.

The mountain region where I served as pastor was well known for its production of illegal liquor. The sale and possession of liquor was regulated by "local option," and we lived in a county that had voted dry – in other words, liquor of any kind was illegal in our county.

Both state and local authorities were given the mandate of enforcing that edict. As a conscientious State Patrol Officer, Eddie had apparently attempted to do that, making several arrests and interdicting the flow of illegal liquor.

I learned that one night, as he was walking to his patrol car, he was abducted by several armed men, blindfolded, and taken to a remote location where he met the man who was behind a rather sophisticated bootleg operation which did business in the whole southeastern segment of the state which included our "dry" county.

Once he was before the man, he had been threatened – but not with harm to himself. Instead, they had described in vivid and gross detail what they would do to his family if he did not relent and stop interfering with their operation. In fear for his family, Eddie had agreed to "look the other way."

It became evident that it was shortly after all of this occurred that he had come to me and asked to resign as a deacon. At the time he resigned I could not get a clear reason why he wanted to give up the office. Now it became painfully clear. His tender conscience could not endure being in spiritual leadership while allowing the law he was sworn to uphold be broken.

Soon he began to miss church altogether, and fell into the dangerous condition of a believer out of fellowship with God and estranged from His Word. The words of the Apostle come forcibly to mind, *neither give place to the devil* (Ephesians 4:27), meaning, just don't allow Satan any room to operate in your life.

With the voice of God's Spirit quenched, the support of the Word of God gone, the guilt of conscience and continual vexation of fear overwhelming him, Eddie gave way to the Tempter's voice. Believing Satan's lie that there was no hope and no way out, he took his own life, leaving his wife and children to try to pick up the pieces.

Circumstances, either those of our own making or those into which we are thrust by forces beyond our control almost always play a huge part in the impulse and decision to commit suicide. This became evident in another case I had to deal with.

For about twenty years I directed a ministry that operated a large Christian camp in Northeastern Pennsylvania. The camp operated year-round which necessitated a fairly large staff of people. Our maintenance department alone was comprised of a half dozen people.

One of those people was a man we will call Don (fictitious name). Don was a part of my staff at Camp of the Nations. Technically, he was on the maintenance crew, but he did far more than maintenance. Don was one of the most pleasant people I have ever met. He was not a large man, but well-built and very athletic. He was an excellent rider and sometimes helped with the horse program. Dressed in western wear, he could easily have been mistaken for Roy Rogers, and was just as good looking.

Don came to the camp because of a personal tragedy. His wife had divorced him for another man and Don was devastated. He did everything he could to restore the marriage but to no avail. His wife remained unmoved by his appeals for reconciliation.

He had been personally discipled by a godly pastor in his home area of New York State and eventually began to volunteer at the camp, finally deciding to join the staff. I believe it was just too painful for him to live in proximity to his wife and family and coming to camp gave him a new environment where he could throw himself into the work and try to forget what he could not change.

Don served on the staff for a number of years and endeared himself to all of us by his gracious willingness to do most anything he was asked to do, and more. However, as the years passed, it became increasingly clear that his divorce had taken a toll on his emotional well-being and he suffered from occasional bouts of, what I would describe as, mild depression.

Then one summer we had a rather attractive young woman join the staff from a major metropolitan city down state. She had been strongly recommended and we placed her in the equestrian program working with the horses.

I have often said that camp directors tend to find out in October, what they needed desperately to know in July. This situation was certainly one of those cases. The young woman subtly worked her way into the affections of at least three of the men on staff.

First, a young man of college age working in the same department, then Don, and finally, a married man who was just coming on staff. It was the last of the cases that finally uncovered the situation when the man's wife learned that her husband had been committing adultery with a girl just out of high school.

But before that final case uncovered the situation, I learned that our young lady had invited Don to ride with her on several occasions and that he had done so. I called him in and warned him that while I trusted him completely, the appearance of his being alone on a trail ride with a young single girl was not good.

I had never known Don to respond with anything but gratitude for counsel before, but on this occasion, he acted almost violently, assuring me that there was nothing wrong in the relationship and that he was offended that I would even consider the matter.

I had a strong affection for this dear man and I overlooked his outburst, but told him that in the nature of things, he would have to see that there were several others with them if they chose to ride the horses together.

Unfortunately, I foolishly dismissed the matter, thinking that was the end of it.

It was several months before the situation surfaced with the other man, but I noticed that Don seemed withdrawn and in a deeper depressed state than I had ever seen before. I made a number of efforts to help him through that, taking him with me several times on business matters where we would have time to talk.

In the meantime, Don's mother had come to live with him and I hoped that her presence would lift his spirits – it did not. After about a year, Don began looking for a care facility where he could place his mother. I got involved with him to help him find a really nice facility that would be well-staffed and where she could get the care she needed. Once we had gotten her settled, Don seemed genuinely relieved. His depression seemed to lift, and I thought perhaps we had gotten through the problem.

Friday mornings I always met with the staff for devotions, after which I would meet with each department head separately and review the work to be accomplished in the week ahead. When we met that Friday, Don was not present. When he did not arrive even after the devotional period, I sent my son Phil, who was also on the staff, to see what was keeping Don.

Phil re-appeared a few minutes later, pale and shaking as he told me what he found. Don had taken a shotgun and aiming it at his head, pulled the trigger. It was not pretty.

There were lots of incriminations regarding the tragedy as there always are, but it was not until a few months later that I was able to begin to put the pieces of the puzzle together.

As the truth began to emerge about the other cases that involved the young lady, additional information convinced me that Don had gotten caught in the same trap that at least two other men had. Tender of conscience, and not able to face the shame of what he had done, his guilt led him to desperation and his desperation ended in suicide.

Don's case is not unique. Sexual promiscuity, marital infidelity, and fornication take an awful toll. If the truth were known, far more cases of suicide can be attributed to this kind of behavior than are known. This seems especially true for men.

Men who fall into the trap of adulterous relationships, and who have any sense of propriety at all, are often carried to despair and desperation that ends in suicide, or murder. Well did that ancient writer observe, *Let not thine heart decline to her (an immoral woman's), ways go not astray in her paths. For she hath cast down many wounded: yea, many strong men have been slain by her. Her house is the way to hell, going down to the chambers of death* (Proverbs 7:25 – 27).

Satan, the accuser of the brethren, first tempts and leads the unwary into such situations, then, once the sin is committed, he is relentless in his accusations of guilt and condemnation. Fear of being "found out" drives the person to desperation. Satan plants the thought that the only way out is to end it by suicide, and another tragedy follows the first. And this is particularly effective with those who have a tender conscience. Satan uses circumstances to bring us to despair and death.

Before we end the discussion of the effect of circumstances on suicide we need to address the issue of the alternative, that is, in circumstances like I have described in the preceding two cases, what could either of these men have done?

Someone has well observed that we cannot always control our circumstances, but we can always control our response to our circumstances. Whether we meet our circumstances with despair, or whether we meet them with faith will determine the final outcome.

For the believer there is always the faithful promise of God, *There hath no temptation taken you but such as is common to man: but God is faithful, who will not suffer you to be tempted above that ye are able; but will with the temptation also make a way to escape, that ye may be able to bear it* (1 Corinthians 10:13).

There is always another way – God's way, out of difficult circumstances, even those of our own making. That way may not be easy, it may be costly, but it will always be right. As the wise man once said, *Trust in the LORD with all thine heart; and lean not unto thine own understanding. In all thy ways acknowledge him, and he shall direct thy paths* (Proverbs 3:5, 6).

Remember, that in both of these situations, there was a compromise with sinful behavior that preceded the tragedy. God has provided a sufficient path out of such situations. It begins with confession to God of what we have done. *If we confess our sins, He is faithful and just to forgive us our sins, and to cleanse us from all unrighteousness* (1 John 1:9).

Then God tells us to *Walk in the Light as He is in the light* (1 John 1:7). What that means is to live a life of transparency. If we have committed a wrong, confess it and seek to make it right.

Obviously, that is never easy and the more complicated the situation, the more difficult the way out. But God assures us that there is a way and that He will walk with us through it.

Suppose either of the men I have spoke about would have followed that counsel. Suppose Don would have told me the truth when I confronted him. It would have been embarrassing and painful, but I could have helped him work through it. Instead, trying to hide sin leads to internal agony and conflict and in this case ended in suicide.

Remember another piece of counsel from the Almighty – *He that covereth (tries to hide) his sins shall not prosper: but whoso confesseth and forsaketh them shall have mercy* (Proverbs 28:13).

Chapter Four

OTHER FACTORS:
THE MIND – HOW WE THINK

As I was writing this, I was watching a documentary on the Second World War produced by NBC. In it, a number of military men told their stories of the horrors of that war. One man told of killing a young German soldier who had raised his rifle only a few feet from him.

After killing him, the sight of that blue-eyed youth fixed itself on his memory so that he could not forget him. For years he would relive the episode in his dreams. Then he related how the thought came of committing suicide to relieve himself of the guilt. He said, "Sometimes it was as if a voice spoke to me and even told me in detail how to take my life."[29]

While neither the soldier relating the experience, or the narrator recognized what was occurring, those with spiritual understanding can recognize clearly the Satanic attempt to destroy yet another of his victims.

With fewer and fewer of our young military having strong biblical foundations for their lives when they enter the service, it is no wonder we are experiencing a terrible surge of suicide cases among both active and retired service personnel.

It has been said that, "War is hell." While we would have to debate that in technical terms, it is certainly true that war is as bad as it gets this side of hell. The experiences, scenes and even the smells of combat and carnage are forever indelibly etched upon the hearts and minds of those who go through it, and they become ready fodder for Satan to ignite in his continuing desire to destroy us.

The first, and often the most difficult step, is to understand where the temptation to suicide originates.

I have spoken to high school students that have either contemplated or attempted suicide. In almost every instance, they have told me of hearing voices urging them to kill themselves, or that they had experienced such a strong compelling obsession to do so that they could think of nothing else.

One youngster whose life was saved by intervention described herself in these words, "I'd lost my ability to think clearly or solve problems, and ended up trapped in a tunnel where I thought only about escape, until self-destruction became the only light I could see." [30]

Almost by definition, suicide points to underlying psychological vulnerability. The thinking behind it is often obsessive and then impulsive. A person can be ruminating about suicide for a long time and then one night something ordinary—a botched quiz, a breakup, a lost business contract, or some put-down (either verbally or on social media), leads him or her to perform the act.

It may be argued by academia that this compulsion is simply, "a form of mental illness." Well, I would observe that such a statement is a stranglehold on the obvious. It is certainly not mental health!

But to make the observation that suicidal obsession is mental illness, is to beg the question of both the source and the cure for the problem.

There is something (or someone), who is whispering in our ears, "take your own life," "kill yourself," "you'd be better off dead," and a thousand other dangerous messages. And it doesn't matter whether the problem is in some school in the ghetto, or at Silicon Valley's schools.

It was there, in Silicon Valley, that Ron Gillenson, who has helped oversee the mental-health program at one school said, "School counselors remained overwhelmed and overloaded with an influx of kids considered high risk." Twelve percent of Palo Alto high-school students surveyed in the 2013–14 school year reported having seriously contemplated suicide in the past 12 months. [31]

After a chain of student suicides one counselor reported, "At Gunn, the scariest thing kids told me is that now, in one student's phrasing, "suicide is one of the options."[32]

Suicide must NEVER be "one of the options."

So, what we have seen is that this issue involves a battle that is taking place in the mind. Suicide always begins there.

We are going to address more fully the question of the control of the mind, but one thing absolutely essential is communication, and I mean open communication especially within the family unit. Parents need to know what their kids are thinking.

Several years ago, after a school assembly program, I got the following letter from a parent of one of the students that had attended that assembly. I'm always thankful when a parent understands that suicide is something that can happen in their own family. The mother who sent me this note was a nurse and she wrote;

> .. We have two daughters at the Academy. I was glad when L. came home from school to hear that you were touring with a program on suicide. At times, I think that Satan has rocked believers to sleep thinking that these things (suicide, abortion, drugs) aren't a problem to Christians.
>
> Working in a hospital, my life isn't as sheltered as some people. Time after time I watch kids brought into the emergency room after a suicide attempt. Once we have done what we need to do medically, the family is brought back in.
>
> The mother stands there not talking, with her heart broken in two and not knowing what to say and the child at that point isn't talking either. It's a scene that makes you want to cry. What it makes me do is cry to the Lord asking that these lines of communication might remain open between myself and my girls.
>
> Thank you, Dr. Shade for your help.

Chapter Five

THE ENIGMA OF SUICIDE

Obviously, the challenge before us is not only to define and understand the problem and the contributing factors to the problem, but to find ways to alleviate the problem. "Suicide Intervention" is a term commonly used to refer to activities that prevent suicides and behaviors closely associated with suicide including thinking about or considering taking one's own life.

If you go on-line or Google the subject you will find an amazing amount of material, articles, books, agency reports, statistics, and recorded attempts at intervention.

With the recent emphasis on bullying as a cause for suicide, some tremendous efforts have been put forth. Even Michelle Obama, the former First Lady, has taken up the cause.

So, with all that is going on, how are we doing at preventing (or even reducing) the incidence of suicide?

Here are summaries of two recent studies:

• A meta-analysis of bullying prevention programs found that although "school bullying interventions may produce modest positive outcomes, they are more likely to influence knowledge, attitudes, and self-perceptions rather than actual bullying behaviors." 33

• A research review concluded that interventions employing classroom curricula or social skills training <u>did not decrease bullying</u>.34

The facts are very clear – they are stubbornly clear, we are losing the battle. Our best efforts and our brightest minds have not found the solution for this enigma.

What about the other categories of vulnerability such as failure, or the fear of failure, or stress caused by parental (and personal) expectations? In the Silicon Valley cases, the schools were, "stalked with suicide-prevention experts: professionals from Stanford and others who had dealt with this phenomena for years."35

After the 2009–10 cluster, the school district had put together a comprehensive post-suicide "toolkit" and trained the staff on what to do to help prevent another cluster from developing.

In Palo Alto, the community has marshaled legions of experts on sleep, stress, social contagion, and any other potentially relevant subject. Yet, in spite of all that was done, according to their own report, school counselors remained overwhelmed and overloaded with an influx of kids considered high risk and the suicide syndrome continued unabated.

David Lester, a psychology professor at Stockton University, in New Jersey, and an authority on suicide, recently confessed, "I'm expected to know the answers to questions such as why people kill themselves," he said. "Myself and my friends, must often, admit that we really don't have a good idea why it happens."36

When all of the many factors that contribute to the act of suicide have been explored, it is both amazing, and appalling to me, that the one factor that is the single common denominator in every case is largely overlooked.

I have read a number of books on the subject of Suicide by good and even godly men who would testify to a fervent belief in the Scriptures, and yet, who seemingly miss this one commonality in every case of suicide.

Some of these writers examine the phenomena of suicide from every possible angle, and yet wittingly or unwittingly avoid, or overlook this one essential and ever-present element.

What is that element? It is the element of the spiritual – it is the element of demonic involvement and activity.

Now to even suggest something like demons in this "P. C." environment is enough to raise the scorn and derision of the average man on the street not to mention the academic elite. The idea conjures up specters of ghosts and goblins and witch hunts right out of the Dark Ages.

Regardless, however, of the reaction of the academic elite, the standard of Truth for me is always the Word of God, and I have found it to correspond to reality and life at every level. After all, I did not expect this book to be the next best seller in the pages of *Psychology Today*.

Let me be perfectly forthright and candid – It is my firm and honest conviction that there is a demonic dimension present in every case of suicide, without exception.

I recognize, of course, that such a statement falls clearly out of the realm of accepted theories, but if it is unconventional (and I know that it is), let me explain why I am so firmly convinced that it is true.

The Nature of Our Spiritual Enemy

In my discussion of Satan in the World Wide Bible Institutes (WWBI), Course on Angels and Spirits, I examine the following descriptive titles of Satan:

> "Satan is a destroying spirit. He is called in Scripture: *The Devil, Beelzebub* (which is the Egyptian name for the fly-god and means "the restless one"); *an angel of light* (2 Corinthians 11:14); *a roaring lion* (1 Peter 5:8); *the wicked one* (Matthew 13:19; 1 John 5:19); *a murderer and a liar* (John 8:44); *the prince of the power of the air,* and *the spirit that now works in the children of disobedience* (Ephesians 2:2); *The Great Red Dragon* (Revelation 12:3); *that old serpent* (Revelation 20:2); *the tempter* (Matthew 4:3); *Apollyon (which means Destroyer* Revelation 9:11); *the prince of this world* (John 14:30); *the god of this world* (2 Corinthians 4:4); *the accuser of our brethren* (Revelation 12:10); *your adversary* (1 Peter 5:8); *the enemy* (Matthew 13:39; Psalm 7:1-5); and *a strong man armed* (Luke 11:21)."[37]

Now if you have taken the time to look carefully at the Scriptural references given above, you will see that Satan is real and personal and a murderer and liar (John 8:44), the eternal enemy of God, angels and man. He loves no one but himself and will use anyone or anything to gain his ends.

He delights in destruction, misery and death, deceit, murder and fear, and is utterly and totally malicious in everything he does.

He is revealed as the head of a great organization of spirit creatures (principalities and powers), who pay him allegiance and worship him, and who together seek to bring to pass the program he began long ago as recorded in Isaiah 14:13-14 where he acted to depose God and reign supreme. He is incorrigible and uncompromising in his goals and wholly unscrupulous in his methods and means.

Satan attacks by tempting us to evil, then laying a heavy burden of guilt on our consciences over the evil he tempted us to do.

He is ever casting doubts concerning God and His Word, perverting the truth, corrupting the nations, possessing individuals to bring about the destruction of themselves and others, tormenting the mind with unclean and horrible suggestions, controlling the governments of the world to his own ends and generally blocking, resisting, perverting, subverting, and opposing God, His people and His plan in the world.

And we should never forget that he is doomed, along with all those angelic beings which obey him and all those men who remain under his control, to the eternal torments of the Lake of Fire where he will not reign but be cast to the lowest place and totally humiliated and fiercely tormented forever and ever (Matthew 25:41; Revelation 20:10-15).

Now if all of that is true, and it is, for the sake of our discussion we need to notice especially the devil's delight in destruction and death. It is alluded to several times in the statements above and is evident as we look at the record of recent events in our time.

In an article entitled, "Satanism Thriving In North America," the *Christian Inquirer* reviewed a recent program of 20/20 aired on the ABC Network. In it, 20/20 "gave horrifying reports of young children who were forced to participate in actual human sacrifices." According to the reporter, "Police stated that the satanic element of such crimes is normally suppressed by local investigators." [38]

I met many teens during those assembly programs that were crying out. One of them wrote,

> *I'm writing to tell you how incredibly impressed I was with the program this weekend! I found that God does have a will in my life thanks to God speaking through you.*
>
> *Many times, as you preach I find that it seems like you are talking directly to me. In this last year, I've had two friends commit suicide, and in this last week four of my "football buddies," got in a car accident and two died.*
>
> *I have a friend at school, his name is G. He tried to commit suicide last year but he didn't succeed. They put him in a mental institution for a couple of months and he came out not wanting to die.*
>
> *But this year he is showing some signs again and I'm really worried about him. I talked to him about God, but he said, "You believe what you believe and I'll believe in what I want." He says he belongs to the church of the devil and Satan is his master, and all this other nonsense.*
>
> *Please, if you would send me some materials that would help me deal with these problems it would be much appreciated. T.S.*

Aaron Klien is the host of "Investigative Radio" on New York's WABC radio station. Klien did an in-depth look at the Sandy Hook killings and then expanded his research to look at a number of other similar incidents that occurred over the previous years. His findings are revealing and confirm the connection we make here of a dark spiritual involvement in death and destruction.

Adam Lanza was the Sandy Hook assassin. On December 14, 2012, Adam began by shooting his mother, Nancy Lanza, in the head at her home in Newtown, Connecticut. He then traveled to the nearby Sandy Hook Elementary School, where he shot and killed 20 students between the ages of 5 and 10, and six adult workers. According to police reports, Lanza then turned the gun on himself, fatally shooting himself in the head. [39]

Trevor L. Todd, a former classmate of Lanza's, told media that Lanza worshiped the devil and had an internet page dedicated to Satan. Klien asked the obvious question, "Is Adam Lanza's reported devil worship a missing link that could help explain what motivated the Sandy Hook gunman to carry out the school house massacre?" [40]

Klien then proceeded to look at some of the similar cases before Sandy Hook. He found that, "Although largely underreported, Satanic subculture and so-called devil worship has been a factor in numerous other mass killings." [41]

Klien then looked at the famous case of the "Batman" killings in July 2012, at the Century movie theatre in Aurora, Colorado. At his trial, Holmes was convicted on 24 counts of murder and 140 counts of attempted murder for the 2012 Aurora shooting that killed 12 people and injured 70 others. Holmes was arrested shortly after the shooting and jailed without bail awaiting trial. Following this, he was hospitalized after attempting suicide several times while in jail.

Klien discovered that Holmes was obsessed with the Batman character, "Joker," and modeled himself after him. In various Batman movies, including the recent Dark Knight series, the Joker's calling card, is a picture of the devil.

Klien explains, "In the 1989 Batman film, the Joker character, played by Jack Nicholson, is first recognized by Batman as the perpetrator of his parents' murder after the Joker asks Batman, 'Do you ever dance with the devil in the pale moonlight?' Batman has a flashback to when his mother and father were murdered by a man who asked the same question." [42]

As Klien continued his research, he discovered that, "The theme of so-called devil worship and Satanic-style "Goth" subculture has cropped up in numerous other mass shootings, although in some cases the phenomenon may have been under-reported or entirely unreported." [43]

Notice that both murder and suicide (or attempted suicide) were present in both of the cases cited, and, as Klien suggests, the press just doesn't get it. It never occurs to them or the police that there might be something very real and very powerful behind all of this.

Right after the 1999 Columbine High School massacre, there were widespread reports that killers Eric Harris and Dylan Klebold were involved in Goth subculture. Though some have debated this, reading the reports by the psychiatrists that researched all of Harris' writings, habits, posts, etc., one cannot be appalled by their conclusions. They found him characterized by rage, contempt, and a "messianic-grade superiority complex" as well as a total lack of remorse or empathy. The study concluded that he lied constantly for the shear pleasure of "duping his hearers." [44]

These are certainly characteristics of Satan, and whether he was actually involved in Satanism himself, one cannot forget that his first victim was Rachel Scott, a Christian with a vibrant testimony, or that he asked her if she "still believed in God?" before firing the final and fatal shot after she affirmed that she did.

Here again, there was inexplicable murder mayhem and finally suicide, as both perpetrators took their own lives.

Perhaps the most infamous shooting spree related to Satanic symbolism is one carried out by the Manson family in 1969. Manson was found guilty of conspiracy to commit the murders of Sharon Tate and Leno and Rosemary LaBianca carried out by members of his group at his instruction. Tate, married to film director Roman Polanski, was eight-and-a-half months pregnant when she was murdered in ritualistic style in her home by Manson's followers in 1969.

There is the case of the 1980s serial killer Ricardo "Richard" Ramirez, who was dubbed the "Night Stalker" by the news media. Many of his victims were killed in ritualistic style and had various Satanic markings carved into their bodies.

Finally, Klien concludes that, "There have been a slew of other murders in the U.S. reportedly tied to devil worship, and lists such additional examples as Sean Sellers (who testified that he had read the "Satanic Bible" more than a hundred times), and Jim Hardy, the president of his high school student council, who bludgeoned to death Steven Newberry as part of what Hardy and three other teens claimed was a Satanic ritual." [45]

You might ask, but what does this have to do with the subject of suicide itself? Aren't you going outside the perimeters of the subject when you invoke extreme cases like this?

I come back to the nature of Satan as revealed in Scripture. He comes to *kill, to steal and to destroy.* Satan delights in destruction and death and I believe there is ample evidence that he is active in every case of suicide.

Scripture records a long list of cases of people who either committed suicide, or who were urged to do so by spiritual powers, and we would do well to learn from what those cases reveal.

We are going to do just that in the next chapter. I think you will find these biblical instances, both interesting and enlightening.

Chapter Six

THE BIBLE RECORD

Let's visit just a few of the examples in Scripture that demonstrate Satan's desire to bring about despair, destruction and death, and see how these reveal something about the subject at hand.

Job
One of the clearest revelations of Satan's desire for our destruction is his attack on Job. Job was indeed protected by the Sovereign hand of God and Satan could only touch him by obtaining permission from God to do so.

But it is also clear that Satan desired, yes, even delighted in Job's suffering. Read at least the first two chapters of the book. When Satan had done everything possible to bring Job into a condition of utter despair and found he could not, he prompted Job's wife to suggest that Job *"curse God and die."*

The struggle to understand what was happening and why, is played out chapter by chapter much the same way that the same struggle is played out in hearts and minds today, but the actors are never given the privilege of peering behind the scenes to see the perpetrator of Job's suffering.

However, the biblical record does not leave us in that state of uncertainty. God has pulled back the curtain for us to see Job's enemy and ours, and it is inexcusable for us to continue a pointless debate looking for answers to why we are going through the circumstances that would drive us to desperation, when the answer is revealed to us with such clarity in the pages of Scripture.

We have an enemy that seeks to, *steal and kill and destroy!* Once we get hold of that, we can begin to fight back, rather than sink into ever deeper despondency and despair.

One thought that should give us some satisfaction is the realization that Satan chose a man who was significant to God to try to destroy. Perhaps you too may be significant and that is why he attacks you.

Saul

Saul is another case where the connection to the evil one is clear. Saul forsook God and the voice of His prophet and turned instead to the witch of Endor (1 Samuel 28). The Scripture tells us that she had a *familiar spirit.* Basically, that means she had a demon that transmitted information using her as his medium.

What happened on the particular occasion when Saul engaged her was completely irregular as the story clearly indicates. The woman was terrified as the actual spirit of Samuel was allowed to appear and communicate, not through her as a medium, but directly to Saul.

Nevertheless, as Samuel's message made clear, Saul had opened himself to demonic attack and experienced an overwhelming despair the next day as the battle tilted against him. In utter hopelessness, he thrust himself through with his own sword, thus ending his life in an act of suicide.

Whether or not the final blow was struck by the Amalekite (2 Samuel 1), or whether the fellow fabricated his story in the hope of gaining some reward from David, the fact remains that Saul took his own life and once again, Satan is clearly involved.

Ahithophel

Ahithophel was a counselor to David and the Scriptures say some remarkable things about him. In 2 Samuel 16:23 we read that, *the counsel of Ahithophel, which he counselled in those days, was as if a man had enquired at the oracle of God: so was all the counsel of Ahithophel both with David and with Absalom.*

Undoubtedly, Ahithophel was a brilliant and gifted person. Jewish tradition says that he was the Grandfather of Bathsheba, whom David had taken and committed adultery with. If so, he would have had some reason for his evident hatred toward King David, but the connection is not clear enough to be dogmatic.

Nevertheless, when Absalom rebelled against his father and attempted a takeover of the government, Ahithophel sided with the rebel and became his chief counsel. Ahithophel even offered to lead a troop of men to assassinate David and thus destroy any chance for him to return to power.

Only God could defeat his counsel and his intent and He did so through the counter counsel of David's friend Hushai.

The result is recorded in 2 Samuel 17:23, *And when Ahithophel saw that his counsel was not followed, he saddled his ass, and arose, and gat him home to his house, to his city, and put his household in order, and hanged himself, and died, and was buried in the sepulchre of his father.*

While the case of Ahithophel may not be as clear as some other cases, it is obvious that the Great Destroyer gripped this otherwise brilliant man with fear and with a loss of face, and his pride allowed him no alternative but to destroy himself.

The Temptation of Christ
We turn next to the temptation of Christ Himself. Luke records it clearly in Luke 4:9–12. In the last of the temptations, Satan took Christ and set him on a pinnacle of the temple.

Josephus says that the pinnacle rose 180 feet from the courtyard. Whether that exact figure is correct, it was undoubtedly a precipitous height and one which could easily give any normal person an overwhelming sense of vertigo.

It is amazing to me how many commentators seem to think that if Christ would have followed Satan's urging, He would have "floated down to the courtyard without harm." That was what Satan suggested, but clearly that is not what would have happened.

Christ understood that to obey Satan's prompting would have been to "put God to the test," or as the KJV translates it, to "tempt God." This is something Scripture plainly forbids as Christ Himself pointed out.

Thus, to have done what Satan suggested would have been to have sinned and to have removed the Father's protection and most likely to have fallen to His death. In other words, Satan actually was tempting Christ to commit suicide.

The commentator John Gill observes this clearly in the following; *Let it be observed, that Satan did not offer to cast him down himself; for this was not in his power, nor within his permission, which reached only to tempt; and besides, would not have answered his end; for that would have been Satan's own sin, and not Christ's: <u>accordingly,</u>*

we may observe, that when he seeks the lives of men, he does not attempt to destroy them himself, but always puts them up to doing it themselves. 46

Well said! How many people have acted upon the temptation to harm themselves, presuming that, "if God loves me, He will not let me die." Foolish and presumptuous thought – *Thou shalt not tempt the Lord thy God* (Luke 4:12). Nevertheless, the point of this is to note once again that Satan is involved in this urging to suicide.

The Demoniac (Legion)

Probably one of the most notable individuals we meet in Scripture is the demoniac of Gadara. All the Synoptics record this incident, but perhaps Mark tells it best for our purposes.

> *And they came over unto the other side of the sea, into the country of the Gadarenes. And when he was come out of the ship, immediately there met him out of the tombs a man with an unclean spirit, Who had his dwelling among the tombs; and no man could bind him, no, not with chains: Because that he had been often bound with fetters and chains, and the chains had been plucked asunder by him, and the fetters broken in pieces: neither could any man tame him. And always, night and day, he was in the mountains, and in the tombs, crying, and cutting himself with stones.*
>
> *But when he saw Jesus afar off, he ran and worshipped him, And cried with a loud voice, and said, What have I to do with thee, Jesus, thou Son of the most high God? I adjure thee by God, that thou torment me not. For he said unto him, Come out of the man, thou unclean spirit.*
>
> *And he asked him, What is thy name? And he answered, saying, My name is Legion: for we are*

many. And he besought him much that he would not send them away out of the country. Now there was there nigh unto the mountains a great herd of swine feeding.

And all the devils besought him, saying, Send us into the swine, that we may enter into them. And forthwith Jesus gave them leave. And the unclean spirits went out, and entered into the swine: and the herd ran violently down a steep place into the sea, (they were about two thousand;) and were choked in the sea (Mark 5:1-13).

At first glance, it may not be apparent that this is a suicidal situation, but it is. Notice what the demons were driving the man to do. He was naked (as the other Gospel writers inform us), and was always, *crying out and cutting himself with stones.* These demons were clearly destructive spirits that were driving the man to suicide.

His superhuman strength, (*he could not be bound with chains*), testifies to full blown demon possession. All of his actions demonstrated an intense, insatiable desire for self-destruction. Why he had not already accomplished killing himself may have been, at least in part, to the attempted concern and intervention of his friends who were trying to bind and restrain him to protect him from himself.

I think these friends sometime mirror the futile efforts we make to turn people from self-destruction in our day. The suicidal syndrome was immediately broken when the real source of trouble was exposed and eliminated.

The final evidence we have in this record that these were destructive spirits is the reaction of the swine. As soon as those same demons possessed the swine the entire herd *ran violently down a steep place into the sea* and were drowned.

Sooner or later these demons would have done the same to this man, and sooner or later spirits today will do the same to those they torment unless they are recognized and dealt with.

The Demon-Possessed Son
This particular case is recorded in all three of the Synoptic Gospels - only John omits it. The three records taken together give us the greatest amount of information.

Matthew describes the son's condition like this; ***he is lunatick*** (selēniazomai***), and sore vexed: for ofttimes he falleth into the fire, and oft into the water*** (Matthew 17:15).

Mark says; ***And wheresoever he taketh him, he teareth him: and he foameth, and gnasheth with his teeth, and pineth away:*** (Mark 9:18).

Medical Doctor Luke adds; ***Without warning a spirit takes control of him, and he suddenly screams, goes into convulsions, and foams at the mouth. The spirit mauls him and refuses to leave him*** (Luke 9:39 ASV)

Taken together the evidence is clear that a demonic spirit was trying to get this boy to destroy himself. It took Jesus authority to release him from the demon's grasp.

Need we say it again, Satan comes to steal, to kill and to destroy. It is the factor we so often miss and apart from understanding it, we cannot understand the spiritual dimension in suicide.

Judas
The evidence for satanic involvement in the betrayal and suicide of Judas is laid out so clearly in Scripture that it is inescapable. Why then are we so resistant to recognizing

the same forces at work in the phenomena of suicide today?

As early as John 6:64 – 71, Jesus had revealed that there was one in their band that was not a believer, that is, had not truly submitted himself to Christ in faith. He further spoke of Judas as "a devil," thus indicating that his actions were controlled by demonic spirits.

Judas did not possess the outward signs of a man given over to Satan. He was so trusted that he was made the treasurer of the twelve. However, even in this we get a glimpse of his real character in what he was doing.

In John 12:5, 6, Judas reacted strongly against Mary's act of worship in pouring out the ointment with these words: *Why was not this ointment sold for three hundred pence, and given to the poor?*

John then reveals to us the motive behind Judas' words: *This he said, not that he cared for the poor; but because he was a thief, and had the bag, and bare* (away) *what was put therein.* So Judas was already concealing theft from the others.

In John 13:2, we read a clear declaration of Satan's involvement: *the Devil, now having put into the heart of Judas Iscariot, Simon's son to betray him . . .* So, the impetus for this horrendous crime was Satan himself – but he found a ready pawn in the faithless Judas.

Luke records it like this; *Then entered Satan into Judas surnamed Iscariot, being of the number of the twelve. And he went his way, and communed with the chief priests and captains, how he might betray him unto them. And they were glad, and covenanted to give him money. And he promised, and sought opportunity to betray him unto them in the absence of the multitude* (Luke 22:3 – 6).

So, we see that from the beginning, Satan was behind the scenes manipulating Judas into position to betray the Savior. Ultimately, Satan took over completely as Judas yielded himself ever further to his control.

Frankly, the evidence seems to suggest that Judas did not think of his betrayal as fatal for Christ. He had seen Jesus walk away from several attempts on His life before this without harm. The Gospel of John notes these with the words, *for His hour was not yet come* (John 7:30; 8:20).

Apparently, Judas thought that he could betray Christ, add some additional money to the treasury (over which he presided and from which he stole), and that Christ would once again walk away unharmed. I think that is clearly what we learn as we read Judas' reaction to Christ's arrest, and condemnation.

Then Judas, which had betrayed him, when he saw that he was condemned, repented himself, and brought again the thirty pieces of silver to the chief priests and elders, Saying, I have sinned in that I have betrayed the innocent blood. And they said, What is that to us? see thou to that. And he cast down the pieces of silver in the temple, and departed, and went and hanged himself (Matthew 27:3 – 5).

Notice the sequence again. Satan tempts to sin. This he did in first tempting Judas to steal from the bag in his possession. As the person yields, Satan tempts to ever greater and more dangerous exploits of evil.

Note that there is also deception here. Judas was deceived into thinking that he could betray Christ and that Christ would (as He had in the past), simply walk away unharmed. Judas was obviously subject to a deep Satanic deception.

Finally, Satan takes control to bring about the greatest sin of all. It is just such a great sin that David wrote about in Psalm 19: *Then shall I be upright and shall be innocent from the great transgression.* Yielding to Satan in the tiniest matter, opens a person to committing *great transgression* (Psalm 19:13).

No wonder Paul wrote, *Neither give place to the devil* (Ephesians 4:27), which the International Standard Version translates, *do not give the devil an opportunity to work.*

Once the victim of Satan's wiles has committed that crime (whatever serious sin it might be to which Satan drew him), Satan then pours on him unbearable accusations of guilt, bringing the person to the depths of despair. Finally, he urges that death is the only release and obsesses the victim with thoughts of self destruction.

Judas' end is vividly recorded in Acts 1:18, *Now this man purchased a field with the reward of iniquity; and falling headlong, he burst asunder in the midst, and all his bowels gushed out.*

Tradition says that he hung himself by leaping from the wall of the Temple. Apparently, the rope broke and his body burst as it fell on the very plot of ground the High Priests had purchased to bury strangers (uncircumcised Gentiles) in with the thirty pieces of silver Judas had returned.

The historian, Alford Edersheim, has a profound insight when he writes, "The demonized were incapable of separating their own consciousness and ideas from the influence of the demon, their own identity being merged, and to that extent lost, in that of their tormentors." [47]

So, in other words, all those suggestive thoughts of self-destruction – where did they originate? From the same Satanic source, we see so clearly in the case of Judas. Why should we doubt that Satan is thus involved in every case of suicide?

In retrospect, does it not also seem evident that God has had these specific cases recorded in His Word, so that we might understand the true nature of the phenomena of suicide? Perhaps our inability to get to the bottom of this is due to our refusal to look in the right places.

Chapter Seven

THERE IS A STRATEGY

One question that has been asked me is why I think Satan has any interest in or involvement with suicide. To answer that question, we need to understand Satan's overall strategy as revealed in Scripture.

What I am about to say is basic and may be very familiar to you. But unless we lay these basic truths out clearly in the beginning, we will not be able to show eventually how victory over suicide (and every form of Satanic deception) is possible.

Satan's first goal is to keep men and women from coming to Christ for salvation. Consider the word pictures given in the first chapter of the book of Colossians. The Apostle writes, *(God) hath delivered us from the power of darkness, and hath translated us into the kingdom of his dear Son: In whom we have redemption through his blood, even the forgiveness of sins* (Colossians 1:13, 14).

The picture is that of someone being held captive in what the Apostle calls, *the kingdom of darkness.* This can be none other than that kingdom over which Satan has power – it is his dark kingdom in which the person is imprisoned. A similar passage is found in Ephesians chapter two.

And you hath he quickened, (brought to life), *who were dead in trespasses and sins; Wherein in time past ye walked according to the course of this world, according to the prince of the power of the air* (Satan), *the spirit that now worketh in the children of disobedience. Among whom also we all had our conversation* (manner of life – i.e., the way we lived), *in times past in the lusts of our flesh, fulfilling the desires of the flesh and of the mind; and were by nature the children of* (under) *wrath, even as others* (Ephesians 2:1 – 3).

In these two passages, we are told that those who have believed and trusted Christ are rescued from the power and authority of Satan, and placed into the Kingdom of Jesus Christ.

That implies, and the Ephesians passage clearly teaches, that all people were at one time under Satan's control and part of his kingdom. Whether that is evident in an individual life or not, is not the issue. The fact is, that was our case and the case of every other person born of the seed of Adam.

To rescue a person out of the kingdom involves a practical invasion into the realm of Satan's control (his kingdom), and a removal of those who were formerly under his power and sway. Such an action must necessarily meet with resistance and indeed it does. Spiritual deliverance is as much a real contest as was Israel's deliverance from Pharaoh in Egypt.

If you have ever tried to lead a soul to Christ, you know that it is a spiritual battle in which Satan often employs every tactic he can to avoid that moment when the person places their full faith in the Son of God and is instantaneously and permanently delivered from Satan's control.

Jesus described that battle when He was accused of casting out demons by the power of Satan himself. Jesus responded by saying,

How can Satan cast out Satan? And if a kingdom be divided against itself, that kingdom cannot stand. And if a house be divided against itself, that house cannot stand. And if Satan rise up against himself, and be divided, he cannot stand, but hath an end. No man can enter into a strong man's house, and spoil his goods, except he will first bind the strong man; and then he will spoil his house (Mark 3:23 – 27).

All of these passages (and others) taken together declare plainly that when a person comes to Christ, a deliverance takes place. The person is delivered from Satan's kingdom and Satan's authority. The person receives new life and is delivered from a manner of life that reflects the nature of his former owner – the Devil.

These passages also make clear that such a deliverance does not take place without a battle, and that Satan will resist any time a soul is rescued from his grasp just as Pharaoh resisted Israel's deliverance from bondage.

The Colossian passage gives us the legal grounds upon which God makes claim to the soul that trusts His Son, *in whom we have redemption through His blood* (Colossians 1:14).

The blood of Christ has satisfied every demand a Holy God or a broken Law, or an accusing foe can make against us. The blood answers to it all and demands that the believing sinner be set free.

When a soul is saved God literally enters the house or kingdom of the "strong man" (Satan), binds him with the claims of Christ's redemptive work, and spoils him by rescuing the believing sinner from his grasp. And He does this work through the Holy Spirit and the human agency of His Church, the Body of Christ on earth. That is exactly what He meant when He said, *I will build my Church, and the gates of hell* (the defensive doors of Satan's kingdom), *shall not prevail against it* (Matthew 16:18).

So, it can be authoritatively stated that the first goal of Satan is to retain his power over men and to keep them from being saved. Suicide then becomes one of his methods.

If Satan can so manipulate the mind of an unsaved person so that he will take his own life, he has succeeded in keeping that one from salvation and Christ's kingdom.

Satan's second goal, if he fails in keeping a person from coming to Christ, is to keep the believer from living a productive and victorious life.

Finally, and in line with what we have said before, Satan's ultimate goal is not only a defeated Christian, but a defeated Christian that has so destroyed his own testimony and shamed the cause of Christ that nothing he ever says or does can be used to influence another person to come to Christ. What better way to utterly destroy a testimony than to bring that defeated Christian to commit suicide?

While suicide seems to present an "easy way out," and is, in some societies, looked upon with a sense of romance and heroics, it is anything but that, and I will demonstrate that fact in the next chapter when we **unmask suicide.**

Chapter Eight

SUICIDE UNMASKED

I am convinced that suicide seems an attractive option to some because suicide wears a mask. It is a mask of denial, and it denies the right and true impulses of hope, and of duty, and God, and hell and love. I want us to walk through each of these and pull the mask off the real face of this terrible act.

1. Suicide is the denial of Hope
The false claim of suicide to every person who falls victim to its impulse is that their particular case is without hope. Basically, it says that whatever it is that the person is rebelling about in their life – whether it be poor health, financial loss, intense and seemingly endless pressure, the rejection of people – whatever the situation, the lie that is told to the person going through the problem is that their situation will never change.

This is the motivation behind the cry for legalized euthanasia. It is based on the claim that the suffering being experienced cannot be reversed or borne, so suicide is chosen to "end the pain."

I have lived long enough to see through the mask of that lie. I have seen too many people come back from the very brink of death, and recover to a full and useful life, to believe the lie that there is no hope. We need to remember that there are no terminal cases with God.

I had the privilege some year ago of speaking to a large assembly of the Christian Women's Club in Baltimore, Maryland. Before I spoke, they had a young lady sing and I watched as her friend and accompanist moved her wheelchair to the microphone. She had suffered a tragic accident, and was a quadriplegic, but she had a wonderful smile and sang beautifully.

That was many years ago, and today Joni Erickson Tada has a worldwide ministry and has helped multiple thousands of people with handicaps learn how to respond in faith to their circumstances and live triumphantly. Thank God, she didn't allow the Enemy of souls to persuade her that her handicapped life was not worth living, or to take her own life in a fit of self pity.

When I spoke in school assemblies, I used to relate what some of the children that we had taken into our Teen Encounter Centers had gone through in their lives. We had three of these centers and housed and ministered to a total of 142 resident teens over a twelve-year period, so we had plenty of exposure to what some of them had suffered.

During the assemblies, I asked, "How many of you have had to watch as your desperate mother poured a can of gasoline over herself and lit a match? How many of you have been forced to eat off the floor or to literally sleep outside in a dog house? How many of you have had a man hold you down while he cut your arm with a razor blade to hear you scream for his own sexual gratification?

Don't you think Satan whispered to every one of those kids that they ought to die? Don't you think he told them their pain was too much to bear – to end it all?

Don't you think they sometimes heard voices that told them to cut their wrists, or take those pills or hang themselves? Yes, they did! And they told me some of what they went through, but they got the victory, and they lived to become happy, productive people.

So, whatever your case may be today, there is hope! Listen to the words of St. Paul as he writes to the Roman Christians:

> *For we are saved by hope: but hope that is seen is not hope: for what a man seeth, why doth he yet hope for? But if we hope for that we see not, then do we with patience wait for it* (Romans 8:24, 25).

> *Now the God of hope fill you with all joy and peace in believing, that ye may abound in hope, through the power of the Holy Ghost* (Romans 15:13).

As long as there is life there is hope. Don't allow Satan to steal away your hope. God will come through for you if you will keep on trusting Him. After all, as the wise man once said, *For to him that is joined to all the living, there is hope: for a living dog is better than a dead lion* (Ecclesiastes 9:4).

I get especially burdened for the many service men who resort to suicide after a career of faithful service to the country. I often think of Clebe McClary, whom I met years ago and have heard speak on a number of occasions.

Clebe's own website tells his story like this;

> "On the night of March 3, 1968, during his 19th reconnaissance mission in Vietnam, Lt. Clebe McClary was critically wounded by an enemy attack. As a result of his bravery under fire and the concern he demonstrated for his men, Clebe was presented the Silver Star and the Bronze Star by the President of the United States. Although Clebe suffered the loss of an eye, an

arm and was told he would never walk again, he never lost the determination, dedication and courage to overcome his circumstances. Clebe McClary is living proof that with the right attitude all things are possible." [48]

Clebe McClary has won scores of men and women to Christ, and influenced thousands to live victorious lives, in spite of his own challenges. Everyone he has influenced thanks God that Clebe did not allow Satan to steal away his hope. Don't forget, <u>suicide is a denial of hope</u>.

2. Suicide is the denial of duty

Secondly, suicide is a denial of duty. What do I mean by that? Every one of us is related to those around us – our lives are mysteriously intertwined with those we touch, and often even with those we hardly know. Scripture puts it like this:

> *For none of us liveth to himself, and no man dieth to himself. For whether we live, we live unto the Lord; and whether we die, we die unto the Lord: whether we live therefore, or die, we are the Lord's* (Romans 14:7, 8).

The Phillips Translation says it like this:

> *The truth is we neither live nor die as self-contained units. At every turn life links us to God, and when we die we come face to face with Him. In life or death we are in the hands of God.*

When we talk about duty, we are talking about your responsibility to others and the influence you have on them. It is a known fact that young people who have had a friend or family member, or someone they looked up to, commit suicide, are far more prone to commit suicide themselves.

This is the basic nature of what has become known as "suicide clusters." It is what happened in the Silicon Valley suicides cited earlier. One kid commits suicide and within weeks, eight others follow.

I used to ask the teens in those assembly programs, "Do you want your younger sister or brother to commit suicide? Do you want your best friend to commit suicide? Do you want someone you may not even know but who looks up to you to commit suicide?" The answer was always, "No." Then I would tell them, think of that when you are contemplating suicide.

Suicide, at its root, is always selfish. Let me quote again from Dr. Charles Solomon in his book, *The Ins & Outs of Rejection*; Suicide is "the ultimate in self rejection – It is the epitome of self-centeredness!" [49]

Remember, the key word is "**self.**" And the more you focus on yourself, the more likely you are to be a candidate for suicide. And when you yield to that dark deed, you will leave the poisonous legacy of your influence on those around you. You have a duty to others – suicide is the denial of that duty.

3. Suicide is the denial of God's rights

When St. John, the writer of the book of Revelation heard the voice that thundered like *many waters* behind him, he heard that voice proclaim, *I am the first and the last: I am he that liveth, and was dead; and, behold, I am alive for evermore, Amen; and have the keys of hell and of death.* (Revelation 1:17b, 18).

Jesus Christ went down into the depths of death and of hell for us and came out victoriously holding the keys. The issues of death and life are in His hands.

Jesus has the keys of death--and He got them through His

death on Calvary. Suicide presumes to take the keys that belong only to Christ – the Prince of Life, and use them without the authority to do so.

Imagine being at a basketball game when suddenly a player from the opposing team decided to end the game on his own terms. To do so he grabbed the whistle from the official's hand, blew it and cried, "game over."

Really? As someone has said, "the game is never over until the last buzzer has sounded," and a player has no right to press the buzzer himself to end the game.

If "it's never over till it's over" were ever in doubt it certainly became extremely clear at the 51st Super Bowl game. The Patriots never put a score of any kind on the board until the third quarter, while the Falcons were leading by three touchdowns (21 points).

The Patriots finally got a 3-point field goal in the third quarter and both teams made touchdowns (but the Patriots missed their extra point). That means the two teams went into the fourth quarter with the Patriots trailing by 19 points, a greater deficit than any team had ever overcome in a final quarter in the history of the Super Bowl.

The fourth quarter changed everything when the Patriots managed to tie the score in the closing seconds of the game and in a sudden-death overtime won by a final score of 34 to 28. Yes, it was unbelievable and probably the game of the century, but it proves once again, "the game isn't over, until it's over," and failure has often been turned into success in the final moments of a game or a life.

This is doubly true for the Christian. Remember, the Christian is God's both by creation and by redemption – we are "twice God's property." Paul says, *You, surely know that your body is a temple where the Holy Spirit lives. The Spirit is in you and is a gift from God. You are no longer your own. God paid a great price for you. So, use your body to honor God* (1 Corinthians 6:19, 20 CEV).

One co-ed told me, "I can't worry about God--this is my problem, it's my body, my future; it's my life – no one else has anything to say about it."

How very different was Job response. When Satan challenged God about Job's faith, God gave him permission to touch everything Job had, and Satan was more than willing to do so.

He took away all of the material goods Job possessed and then all of his children in one day. Job was reduced to a pauper and bereaved of his children in a single blow.

Still Satan was not satisfied. He wanted more, and God granted him the permission to touch Job himself, but warned him, "spare his life."

Soon we find Job reduced to boils and running sores until he cried out, *my soul chooseth strangling, and death rather than life* (Job 7:15).

Nevertheless, when Job's wife suggested that he terminate his life with the words, *Dost thou still retain thine integrity? curse God, and die.* Job's response was, *Thou speakest as one of the foolish women speaketh. What? shall we receive good at the hand of God, and shall we not receive evil* (Job 2:9, 10)?

Job, like most of us, had been the recipient of much blessing from God. Could he now not tolerate suffering and pain? What kind of people are we that we deny God His right over our lives? Shame on us! Shall we receive the blessings of the Lord and shall we refuse trouble? And can we forget that God blessed the latter end of Job's life more than the first?

Remember, God says, *Thou shalt not kill* (Exodus 20:13), and that commandment includes ourselves. Jesus Christ, not you and me, holds the keys to life and to death and He said: *Fear not them which kill the body, but are not able to kill the soul: but rather fear Him* (God) *which is able to destroy both soul and body in Hell"* (Matthew 10:28).

The true fear of God is the greatest deterrent there is to suicide, because the act of suicide denies God's right and authority over us.

And that leads me to the next anomaly of suicide:

4. Suicide is the denial of Hell

When Dexter Gardner recorded those final words just before he fired the fatal shot, he said, "This is Dexter Gardner speaking--I am signing off..." As I noted from his words, he thought he had turned off the set – but what he didn't know was that he had just changed the channel!

Dexter did not end it all – he only propelled himself out into eternity, and if he did not know Christ as his Savior (and there is little evidence he did), his next stop was a place called hell. <u>The only thing death ends is our opportunity to change our eternal destiny</u>.

There is a very poignant verse found in the book of Hebrews – one we do not hear quoted very often these days. It says, *And, as it is appointed unto men once to die but <u>after this</u> the judgment . . .* (Hebrews 9:27). There is something "after this."

Jesus Christ is the Eternal One and He pulled the curtain back on what that "after this" is all about. In St. Luke's Gospel, Jesus said;

> *There was a certain rich man, which was clothed in purple and fine linen, and fared sumptuously every day: And there was a certain*

beggar named Lazarus, which was laid at his gate, full of sores, And, desiring to be fed with the crumbs which fell from the rich man's table: moreover the dogs came and licked his sores.

And it came to pass, that the beggar died, and was carried by the angels into Abraham's bosom: the rich man also died, and was buried; And in hell he lift up his eyes, being in torments, and seeth Abraham afar off, and Lazarus in his bosom. And he cried and said, Father Abraham, have mercy on me, and send Lazarus, that he may dip the tip of his finger in water, and cool my tongue; for I am tormented in this flame. But Abraham said, Son, remember that thou in thy lifetime receivedst thy good things, and likewise Lazarus evil things: but now he is comforted, and thou art tormented. And beside all this, between us and you there is a great gulf fixed: so that they which would pass from hence to you cannot; neither can they pass to us, that would come from thence (Luke 16:19 – 26).

We all agree the rich man was not in hell because he was rich, but because he was self-centered, selfish, and godless.

Suppose the poor man, the beggar, the man who had laid at the gate full of sores, had been the godless one. And suppose he had taken his own life. Would he have been better off in hell? I think not! As bad as his condition was, it was better than that of a man in hell.

The high incidence of suicide in our time is the natural result of the philosophy of existentialism that believes life has no meaning. If I evolved from nothing, and I exist without a purpose, then in death I have nowhere to go. To the existentialist life itself is an absurdity, and death simply ends an absurd existence.

And what if this generation and this culture scorns the idea of a judgment and eternal punishment? *Shall their unbelief make the faith of God without effect? God forbid: yea, let God be true, but every man a liar* (Romans 3:3, 4). Or as the Contemporary English Version puts it; *God tells the truth, even if everyone else is a liar.*

Man's unbelief will not change the facts – there is an "after this" for every individual, and it will be spent in heaven or in hell. But suicide denies the "after this." How do I know? Because Satan always whispers, "it will be better when you are dead – dying will stop the pain" and fools believe him only to open their eyes as the man in Jesus' narrative did, in the flames of hell. Suicide always denies hell.

5. Suicide is a denial of love

I still read those pensive notes that teens handed me after the assemblies.

- "No one cares whether I live or die."
- "Why should I stay here and just take up space?"
- "No one will even notice I am gone."

All, of course, are false, but each is the cry of a broken heart. We live in a broken world and it's not getting better. And all around us are broken hearts, but it is always refreshing when one of those hearts finds healing.

Even preachers sometimes feel like that. Rev. Frank Graeff went through just such a deep and heartbreaking experience. He was to say later that his "whole attitude had become one of despair and defeat" that in turn produced a life which was anything but happy and victorious.

Frank Graeff had lost sight of the One who cares; the One who knows about our heartaches and griefs; the One who is the burden-bearer and has promised never to leave us in such times – the One who loves us with an everlasting love.

Each day saw him slipping, as did Bunyan's Pilgrim (in his classic book, Pilgrim's Progress), deeper and deeper into the "slough of despond and despair" until one day he felt he could stand it no longer. Frank Graeff had come to the end of the road and Satan whispered, "why don't you just end it all?"

In the darkest hour of his extremity, the words of an old hymn began to run through his mind and he softly began to sing a song that had been born out of just such an experience as he was now going through.

It had been written by Joseph Scriven 75 years before. Scriven had gone through just such a devastating experience, when the young lady he loved and to whom he was engaged, drowned a few days before they were to have been married. Out of a heart that was crushed, Scriven wrote:

> *"What a friend we have In Jesus,*
> *All our sins and grief to bear,*
> *What a privilege to carry,*
> *Everything to God in prayer,*
> *Oh, what peace we often forfeit,*
> *Oh, what needless pain we bear,*
> *All because we do not carry,*
> *Everything to God is prayer."*[50]

Frank Graeff could go no further. He dropped to his knees and began to pour out his heavy heart to the One who cared. The peace he had forfeited for so long came flooding back unto his soul and with it a "joy unspeakable and full of glory."

"I know He cares! I know My Savior cares!" shouted the

reclaimed preacher. And so, he too wrote a song — a song called, *Does Jesus Care?* Think about the words –

Does Jesus care
When my heart is pained,
Too deeply for mirth or song,
As the burdens press,
And the cares distress,
And the way grows weary and long?

Does Jesus care
When my way is dark,
With a nameless dread and fear?
As the daylight fades,
Into deep night shades,
Does He care enough to be near?

Does Jesus care
When I've tried and failed,
To resist some temptation strong;
When for my deep grief,
I find no relief,
Though my tears flow all the night long?

Does Jesus care,
When I've said goodbye,
To the dearest on earth to me,
And my sad heart aches
Till it nearly breaks,
Is it aught to Him, does He see?

Oh, yes, He cares,
I know He cares,
His heart is touched with my grief.
When the days are weary,
The long nights dreary,
I know my Savior cares.[51]

The Apostle John wrote:

> . . .*God is love. In this was manifested the love of God toward us because that God sent his only begotten Son into the world, that we might live through him. Herein is love, not that we loved God, but that he loved us, and sent his Son to be the propitiation for our sins* (1 John 4:8 – 10).

A dear godly pastor once told me, "You may die unsaved, but you cannot die unloved," and he was right.

God commendeth his love toward us, in that, while we were yet sinners, Christ died for us (Romans 5:8). Do you want a proof of His Love – look at Calvary.

We are so self-pleasing and selfish that we think if God allows any trouble in our lives, He doesn't love us – Oh! how sinful, how wicked the thought! Suicide is the denial of love.

The things I have written about in this chapter have helped scores of people face the ugly truth about suicide. Suicide is the most selfish, self-centered action any human being can ever take. It is a denial of hope, a denial of duty, a denial of God's rights, a denial of hell, and a denial of love.

If you know someone you think may be contemplating suicide, I wouldn't suggest giving the person this book to read – I would urge you to get permission to read this chapter to him – a chapter in which suicide is unmasked. I think it will help him to see this act for what it really is.

Chapter Nine

THE WARNING SIGNS

If the professional experts haven't had much success in stopping suicide (or even slowing it down), they have provided us with some insights into the sometimes subtle, behavior patterns that often precede the act itself.

I have collected these over the years from a number of sources, so it is impossible for me to cite a single source, but they are generally available now by simply searching online.

Just as certain behaviors and changes occur before events like a heart attack or a stroke, so there are changes that accompany suicide as well and when we see them in a friend or loved one, we need to recognize them as signals that something drastic is about to happen.

When the military looked at this, they actually listed thirty-six "signs of distress" including; Agitation, Alcohol misuse, Anxiety, Apathy, Avoiding recreation, Constant fatigue, Decreased appetite, Decreased libido, Depression, Difficulty coping, Disciplinary problems, Excessive sleeping, Feeling "blah", Feeling guilty, Feeling overwhelmed, Feeling worthless, Financial problems, Hopelessness, Increased appetite, Indecisiveness, Insomnia, Irritability, Loss of interest, Low energy, Low self-esteem, Poor concentration, Poor personal hygiene, Poor work performance, Relationship difficulties,

Restlessness, Sadness, Social isolation, Social withdrawal, Suicidal ideation, Weight gain, Weight loss.[52]

You will find aspects of many of these in the "signs" we discuss below.

I am listing these symptoms in no particular order, and not everyone exhibits all of these, in fact no one would likely exhibit all of them, but when we see even two or three together, we should initiate intervention just as you would if your friend was choking, or having a heart attack.

A few of these really need no comment, but others are things I have personally observed in people who either attempted or committed suicide, and I will make some comments on those items. Also, you will note that some of these are more related to youth, while others may be more observable in adults.

Radical personality change. This can be observable in either youth or adults. In youth, it may take the form of violent or rebellious behavior, or in some cases, even running away. In adults, it can take the form of withdrawal, or an extreme gregariousness. In either form, the thing to note is that it is a departure from the person's usual behavior – they suddenly seem "out of character."

Persistent boredom, difficulty concentrating, or a decline in the quality of work or schoolwork. Obviously, this symptom in relation to schoolwork is descriptive particularly of young people, but the symptom is certainly not exclusive to them. Adults can become bored with their jobs, their careers, their hobbies, even their spouse, and when that happens it is a signal that something is going very wrong.

Not tolerating praise or rewards. This can be proper humility, or it can be a sign that the person is truly having an identity crisis. It can be a sign of self-loathing, but notice again, the emphasis is on **"self."**

Anytime we allow ourselves or others to get caught up in the **self** focus syndrome we are open season for Satan's attacks. All of us are weak and fail more than we should, and Satan knows it.

I remember a professor of mine once saying, "Satan is the accuser of the brethren – and he doesn't even have to lie about us – the truth is bad enough." Well, that is why our focus must be upon Christ and what He can do in us, rather than on ourselves.

Frequent complaints about physical symptoms, often related to emotions, such as stomachache, headache, fatigue, etc. When this persists over an extended period of time and no medical diagnosis can determine a cause, it is time for those closest to the person to try to get to the root of the problem.

I remember a case of a woman who had been very active and vibrant suddenly taking to her bed and complaining of extreme exhaustion and debilitating fatigue. When no physical problem could be found, and after much prayer, she confessed to harboring a bitter spirit.

That night she confessed her sin to God and claimed His forgiveness. The next morning, she was up and as vibrant as ever. However, if her behavior had been ignored, or left unresolved, it is not too much to suppose that something as serious as suicide might have happened.

Withdrawal from friends and family and loss of interest in pleasurable activities. There are certain people who I expect to see from time to time or they will call and tell me what is going on in their lives.

However, if a long gap occurs and I have not heard from them, I become immediately concerned and often try to contact them. Why? Because I know the tendency to communicate when things are going well and stop communicating when things are going badly or there is despondency. This situation sometimes leads to the next sign of trouble . . .

Change in eating and sleeping habits. When either a young person, or an adult, suddenly wants to spend all day (or days) in bed, something is seriously wrong. If it continues it should be cause for concern and intervention. Sometimes the best intervention is getting the person to talk about why they are feeling as they are.

Unusual neglect of personal appearance. Yes, that can be a red flag especially if the person tended to be conscious and careful of their appearance in the past. This behavior signals a low self-esteem and should lead to a friend taking heed to the well-known admonition, "see something, say something."

Drug and alcohol abuse. This is a two-edged sword. Why do I say that? Because drug and alcohol abuse will always lead to depression and in turn depression will often lead to drug and alcohol abuse.

Alcohol, should never become a problem for a Christian, who understands that their body is the temple of the Holy Spirit and the abuse of anything harmful, especially drugs and alcohol should be outside the sphere of their lives completely.

However, even Christians sometimes fall into this sin (as they do any other). Whether saved on not, the only cure I have ever seen is the power of the Holy Spirit on a life wholly yielded to Him.

I had on my staff some years ago a man named Al who had "done drugs" since he was nine years old. By the time he was a teen, he was on heroine. After receiving Christ, he was immediately and completely delivered from all drug use.

I once had his parole officer tell me, "I don't even believe in God, but I can't explain Al. I have never before seen anyone as serious a user as he was suddenly and completely delivered."

Now all of the behaviors we have looked at up until now are serious enough to warrant concern and perhaps intervention. But the next few must be taken very seriously. They are strong signals that I have witnessed in definite cases of suicide or attempted suicide.

Giving verbal hints with statements such as: "I won't be a problem for you much longer," "Nothing matters," "It's no use," "I won't see you again."

The Air Force says, "Many suicide victims communicate their intention to kill themselves verbally and/or behaviorally. In some cases, these communications were clear. For example, one 19-year-old male Airman who had been having serious marital problems told his coworkers he was . . . about to kill himself. Co-workers thought he was just "blowing off steam" and took no action. He subsequently shot himself." [53]

The Air Force followed that story with this admonition, "Every suicidal remark should be taken very seriously; someone's life may depend on it." [54]

Persons who say such things are crying out for someone to stop them. The person does not want to die, but is attempting to see if anyone cares enough to try to intervene.

Don't miss this signal, for if you do, you will carry your own feelings of guilt for not trying to have intervened. When you hear someone make statements as desperate as these – do something.

Putting Your House in Order: This is often misunderstood or misinterpreted. When someone suddenly becomes amazingly generous (most likely a drastic change of character), it might mean he's planning to die and isn't going to need these things anymore.

Suddenly the person begins to put his or her affairs in order – for example, he begins to give away favorite possessions, settle financial accounts and throw things away he formerly cherished. Remember Ahithophel (2 Samuel 17:23).

Questions such as, "aren't you going to need that?" may begin to open the door to discussion and a conversation that might reveal what is really happening inside his mind.

Becoming suddenly cheerful after a period of depression. This one is especially potent to me because this is exactly what I have observed in certain cases.

When a person has been in a depressed state over a long period of time and then suddenly seems to not have a care in the world, you can be sure they have made up their mind to die. The struggle is over, and they have committed themselves to the dark deed.

In the Air Force report on suicide, the report says that, "For many suicide victims, the final stage is the 'calm before the storm.' After making up their minds to commit suicide, they often become tranquil. Those around the victim are likely to correctly interpret this as the victim having solved his or her problems, but incorrectly assume that the solution is a positive one." [55]

In a situation like this, I would address it head-on with something like, "You're planning to kill yourself, aren't you?"

That may seem extreme, and it is, but you don't have time at this point to play psychological games. This person needs to be shocked into the reality of what he is about to do, and needs someone to tell the truth.

Suicide is a terrible and ugly matter that has repercussions both here and in eternity – Don't take it lightly.

Chapter Ten

MY PERSPECTIVE

When I began this book someone asked, "So if you are going to write on a highly technical and social-centric subject like suicide, what credentials do you have? What Sociology degrees do you possess? What degrees in Psychology?"

Fair question – and one for which I have an answer. However, before I even share that with you, I warn you that it will not satisfy all readers. Whether you will accept what I have to say will depend largely on one thing – that is, your attitude toward my information and authority source?

That's right! I will go to an information and authority source that is more qualified than I am to make the assertions that I will make, and the weight my statements will have with you, will depend on your comfort with my authority source. So, let's grapple with that first, before we go any further into the discussion at hand.

Let me identify myself briefly; I am first and foremost a born-again Christian, one who has recognized my own sinfulness, weakness and need and who has placed my entire eternal fate in the hands of Jesus Christ, whom I believe to be the Virgin-born Son of God – God Incarnate.

Jesus Christ died on a Roman cross over two thousand years ago, not just for the sins of the world (in some general sense), but specifically for the sins of each individual – for me – for my sins. And God was so satisfied with the sacrifice He made that He raised Jesus Christ from the dead and has exalted Him at His own right hand.

From His exalted throne in heaven, Jesus offers forgiveness and eternal life to as many as will believe and trust in Him, and He says that whoever calls upon His name will be eternally saved (delivered from eternal separation and torment in the Lake of Fire).

As a teenager, I recognized my need and called upon Jesus Christ. At the time, I was in the hospital, in an oxygen tent, with a heart which doctors said was three times the normal size. I had worked my way into that condition with a wild sinful life and habits I could not bring under control. When I cried out to Jesus, there came a peace and assurance to my soul that I can neither forget nor explain.

Not only did I know that I was forgiven, but I knew that I was free as well. There is an old hymn that expresses it well;

> *He breaks the power of cancelled sin,*
> *He sets the prisoner free,*
> *His blood can make the foulest clean,*
> *His blood availed for me.*[56]

From that moment, I have wanted nothing else than to know Him and to serve Him with my whole life.

After God not only forgave me, but healed me, I went to Bible Institute and College and have spent the past sixty years studying and teaching the Bible – the Word of God.

I have traveled the world, taught in colleges and seminaries, preached in villages and auditoriums, and in every place, I have watched the miracle of transformation happen to those who place their faith in the One who said, *I am the Way, the Truth, and the Life. No man cometh to the Father but by me* (John 14:6).

So, I have no difficulty believing Him when He says things like, *If ye continue in my Word, then are ye my disciples indeed; And ye shall know the <u>truth</u>, and the <u>truth</u> shall make you free* (John 8:31, 32).

Or, *Sanctify them through thy <u>truth</u>: thy Word is <u>truth</u>* (John 17:17). I have made His Word my life-long authority and I have found that it speaks to every experience common to man.

Therefore, these are my credentials – I have spent a lifetime studying, teaching and living the Word of God. The wall of my office may be covered with awards and accolades, but my credentials are simply sixty years of ministry applying the Word of God.

When I come to address any situation in life, the Word of God becomes my authority source and I look at what I am examining through its lens. The subject of suicide is no different. God's Word has the final and only real answer to every problem, including this one.

As for the "Experts", I am reminded of a statement I ran across recently concerning the study of another phenomena that the "experts" have written reams of books and papers about.

The scientific journal said, "In the last 40 years, there has been an explosion of research on this problem as well as a sense that considerable progress has been made. We argue instead that <u>the richness of ideas is accompanied by</u>

<u>a poverty of evidence</u>, with essentially no explanation of how and why this happens." [57]

That statement certainly can be said about the phenomenon of suicide. Scores of books have been written on the subject, but, "<u>the richness of ideas is accompanied by a poverty of evidence, with essentially no explanation of how and why this happens.</u>" – in other words, the experts don't know.

The Air Force certainly has taken the matter seriously and expended considerable assets in order to address the problem. "In May 1996, General Moorman, USAF/CV, commissioned an integrated product team (IPT) composed of all functional areas of the Air Force. He requested General Roadman (HQ USAF/SG), chair the 75-member committee and develop suicide prevention strategies. In spite of the team's best efforts however, suicide remains the second leading cause of death amongst Air Force active duty personnel." [58]

We are living in an era where questions have been raised on great matters like morals, marriage, abortion, euthanasia, gender identity, homosexuality, and life after death. But because our culture has shifted away from a biblical position where there are absolute answers to these questions, we now find ourselves without absolutes and without firm answers.

So, finding ourselves adrift without a position, we attempt by the means of taking polls and measuring what people believe to develop a national consensus.

Frankly, the resulting national consensus, is never anything more than the pooling of human ignorance, superstition and depravity on any given subject. Yet in spite of that fact, through the alchemy of endless repetition, it becomes the "right," and the "politically correct thing to do."

Necessarily, therefore, the biblical position (which will always be at odds with this consensus) becomes the "wrong," and the politically incorrect thing to do and those who adhere to it will therefore be marginalized, ostracized and ultimately persecuted.

But I come to this discussion, not from a "consensus viewpoint," but from a completely different perspective. I join the scores of those who "don't have the answer," but I also come with an absolute assurance that the God who made us knows the answer, and it has pleased Him to reveal that answer to us in His revelation called the Bible.

Therefore, I am content to rely completely on the answers it provides and offer them to you the reader, in full confidence that when applied, they never fail.

In the next three chapters therefore, I will explain what I have called the 3-fold cure for suicide.

Chapter Eleven

STEP ONE:
YOU AND GOD

I wish I had a pill for suicide – and perhaps I do.

I was talking to a doctor several years ago who frankly told me that many (he actually said 80%) of the people he provided medical care for, were "psychosomatically ill." He said, "I don't mean they didn't have anything physically wrong with them, but I believe that most of what was wrong was brought on by emotional distress and a tormented mind."

When I asked him what he thought caused that condition he replied in one word, "Guilt!" I then asked him what pill he prescribed for Guilt? He replied, "Bill, if I had the answer to that, I would have the greatest medical breakthrough in the history of medicine."

"Actually," I told him, "I have the pill and it always works in every situation." When he asked what it was, I told him, "*The Blood of Jesus Christ, God's Son cleanses us from all sin* (1 John 1:7), and guilt."

The whole ugly syndrome of guilt that leads to suicide and a thousand other disasters can be absolutely washed away by simple faith in the cleansing and saving blood of Jesus Christ.

In case that doesn't quite compute with you, let me explain. Sin – any sin, is a crime against God and brings with it the sense of guilt, alienation from God, and the threat of divine punishment. That sense of right and wrong built into us by our Creator, tells us we have transgressed and deserve to be punished.

We know that God is Holy and He will not and can not overlook sin. That is the reason Jesus came into the world. God's justice demanded that sin – all sin, be punished. And the punishment is spelled out clearly in Scripture. *The wages of sin is death* (Romans 6:23), and *Without shedding of blood is no remission* (of sin) (Hebrews 9:22).

So Jesus died in your place and mine, and shed His holy perfect blood for our sin. He became, as John puts it, *The Lamb of God, which taketh away the sin of the world* (John 1:29), and in John's Epistle he says, *And ye know that he was manifested to take away our sins; and in him is no sin* (1 John 3:5).

When we come to Him in believing faith Jesus blood becomes the payment for our sins and God pronounces us free of any and all guilt. When a Christian sins and comes in humble confession of that sin to God, we have His promise, *If we confess our sins, he is faithful and just to forgive us our sins, and to cleanse us from all unrighteousness* (1 John 1:9).

That is why we say that the "pill" that always works to take away guilt is the blood of Jesus Christ. With guilt gone, the desperation that leads to suicide is gone as well.

So, let me talk about what I believe is the three-fold cure of the specter of suicide. Note, I said this is a three-fold cure – one or two steps alone are not enough to ensure the victory, but the three together will not fail.

First, recognize the part Satan plays in suicide and thoughts of suicide. Satan's primary way of attacking us is through our minds. Once he senses any weakness, he will exploit it, and if you are not a child of God through faith in Jesus Christ, you have no real defense against his wiles. As we have already seen, Scripture clearly teaches that Satan has a claim to every one of us from the moment we come into this world, until the moment we are rescued through faith in the Lord Jesus Christ.

That is why it is so important to understand what the Bible teaches. When our first father, Adam, sinned (and yes, Adam is a real historic reality just as sin is a reality), he not only brought guilt upon himself, but upon the entire race. The book of Romans makes that clear.

> *Therefore, as through one man (Adam), sin entered into the world, and death through sin; and so death passed unto all men, for that all sinned* (Romans 5:12 ASV).

Note that the Greek past (aorist) tense occurs in all three verbs in this verse. So, the entire human race is viewed as having sinned in the one act of Adam's sin.

What this verse is teaching is that when Adam sinned, we sinned as well, because God considers us as being "in Adam" when he sinned. Adam is the true, literal head of the entire race and his sin is counted as our own.

Thus, Adam not only broke his relationship to God by his transgression, and the relationship to God of all his posterity, but placed himself under the dominion of the one he obeyed – Satan.

Know ye not, that to whom ye yield yourselves servants to obey, his servants ye are to whom ye obey (Romans 6:16).

That is why the Apostle could write:

> *Wherein in time past ye walked according to the course of this world, according to the prince of the power of the air, the spirit that now worketh in the children of disobedience: Among whom also we all had our conversation in times past in the lusts of our flesh, fulfilling the desires of the flesh and of the mind; and were by nature the children of wrath, even as others* (Ephesians 2:2, 3).

Because of sin, Satan lays claim to us and we are, as we have seen earlier, subjects of his Kingdom. So the question becomes, how can we change that? We certainly do not have the power or the right to self determination in the matter. Once again, Scripture gives us the answer.

> *Giving thanks unto the Father, which hath made us meet* (fit) *to be partakers of the inheritance of the saints in light: Who hath delivered us from the power of darkness* (the kingdom of Satan), *and hath translated us into the kingdom of his dear Son: In whom we have redemption through his blood, even the forgiveness of sins* (Colossians 1:12 – 14).

Thus, we learn that when we, as believing sinners, place our faith and confidence in Jesus Christ, we are immediately released from the kingdom of darkness (Satan's kingdom) and "translated," that is, carried across into the kingdom of God's dear Son (Jesus).

Furthermore, the legal basis for this move was the price of Christ's own blood which paid for our sin and guilt. As long as we had sin on our record, we were guilty and

Satan could claim us. When Christ shed His blood for us, He redeemed us to Himself.

And the Bible teaches that because God was completely satisfied with the offering of the blood of His own Son as a complete and sufficient payment for all sin, of all men, for all time, He proved His satisfaction by raising Christ from the dead – Glorious truth!

But in order for this to be true for you, you must come to Christ in believing faith. That is what God means when He says, *Believe on the Lord Jesus Christ, and you will be saved* (Acts 16:31).

In the matter which we are discussing, taking this step is absolutely crucial. It is the first step in escaping Satan's hold and nothing that I am going to say next will be of any value to you, unless you have knowingly and deliberately trusted Christ as your very own Savior.

If you have never invited Christ into your life to forgive your sin and give you the gift of eternal life, you should do so at once and I want to help you take that step. You can express it something like this:

Dear God, I know that I am a sinner, but I believe that Christ shed His blood for my sins and rose again from the dead to bring me eternal life. I ask you to forgive my sins for Jesus' sake and save me now.

Thank you for loving me, and hearing my prayer, and thank you for saving me.   Amen

God wants you to know for certain that if you are trusting Him, He has saved you and placed you in His kingdom. Look at how clearly the Apostle John explains this:

> *If we receive the witness of men, the witness of God is greater: for this is the witness of God*

which he hath testified of his Son. He that believeth on the Son of God hath the witness in himself: he that believeth not God hath made him a liar; because he believeth not the record that God gave of his Son.

And this is the record, that God hath given to us eternal life, and this life is in his Son. He that hath the Son hath life; and he that hath not the Son of God hath not life. These things have I written unto you that believe on the name of the Son of God; <u>that ye may know that ye have eternal life</u>, and that ye may believe on the name of the Son of God (1 John 5:9 – 13).

Once you have taken this first step, you are a child of God, the purchased possession of His Son, and a citizen of His glorious and everlasting kingdom. Now you have a position and a relationship that can protect you from Satan.

You are His child, born into His family through the new birth, sealed by His Spirit until the day of redemption, His heir and a *joint heir* with Christ Himself, protected by His blood and seated with Him in heavenly places, and you are predestined to be transformed into His image when He comes to call us home. Don't let Satan's lies ever rob you of your exalted position in Christ.

Chapter Twelve

STEP TWO:
STANDING YOUR GROUND

Once you belong to Christ you are on redemption ground – that is, your sin, past, present or future has been atoned for, and nothing can separate you from the love of God. Notice how clear God makes that in the Epistle to the Romans:

> *What, then, can we say about all of this? If God is for us, who can be against us?*
>
> *The God who did not spare his own Son but gave him up for all of us - surely, he will give us all things along with him.*
>
> *Who can bring an accusation against God's chosen people? It is God who justifies them!*
>
> *Who can condemn them? Not Christ Jesus, who died-and more importantly, who has been raised and is seated at the right hand of God and is the one who is also interceding for us!*
>
> *Who can separate us from Christ's love? Can trouble, distress, persecution, hunger, nakedness, danger, or a sword?*

> *As it is written, "For your sake we are being killed all day long. We are thought of as sheep to be slaughtered." No, in all these things we are more than conquerors through the one who loved us.*
>
> *For I am convinced that neither death, nor life, nor angels, nor rulers, nor things present, nor things to come, nor powers, nor anything above, nor anything below, nor anything else in all creation can separate us from the love of God that is in Christ Jesus our Lord* (Romans 8:31 – 39 ISV).

Notice how completely and unreservedly this passage assures our full and eternal acceptance with God through Christ. It is a wonderful passage of assurance – but that is not all that it is.

The passage also implies that we are both the beloved of God and the target of the world and the devil. The world persecutes the Christian and the devil accuses us before God day and night (see: Revelation 12:10). So while we are secure as far as our eternal salvation is concerned, we are also in a conflict while we are here on earth.

This is a winnable contest but we must know the way to victory and deliberately choose to take it. Christians are not defeated because they lack the resources for winning, they are defeated because they ignore those resources or place themselves in a position where they are vulnerable to defeat. This becomes very clear in Paul's words to the Ephesian Christians:

> *Finally, my brethren, be strong in the Lord, and in the power of his might. Put on the whole armour of God, that ye may be able to stand against the wiles of the devil.*

> *For we wrestle not against flesh and blood, but against principalities, against powers, against the rulers of the darkness of this world, against spiritual wickedness in high places. Wherefore take unto you the whole armour of God, that ye may be able to withstand in the evil day, and having done all, to stand* (Ephesians 6:10 – 13).

The first thing Paul tells us in this passage is that we are at war – we are engaged in a conflict. As believers, we must never lose sight of that fact. We have a fierce and determined enemy that is seeking every opportunity to defeat us, and we have to be aware of that fact always.

That enemy is identified as *"the spiritual powers of darkness."* Don't miss this! If Satan cannot keep us from coming to Christ, he will attempt to attack us after we do. That is what is at issue here and if the believer yields at any point, remember Satan's "end game" is to "steal, kill and destroy."

Secondly, the Apostle tells us that we have weapons of warfare that will both protect us (defensively) and allow us to fight back (offensively).

And finally, this part of the passage exhorts us to "take them" – that is appropriate what God has provided for us to both protect ourselves and win the battles we will face.

If we are going to be able to do that, we need to know what God has provided and that brings us to the next portion of this remarkable passage where the Apostle likens our spiritual weapons, to those used by soldiers at that time.

> *Stand therefore, having your loins girt about with truth, and having on the breastplate of righteousness; And your feet shod with the preparation of the gospel of peace;*

> *Above all, taking the shield of faith, wherewith ye shall be able to quench all the fiery darts of the wicked* (one). *And take the helmet of salvation, and the sword of the Spirit, which is the word of God:*
>
> *Praying always with all prayer and supplication in the Spirit, and watching thereunto with all perseverance and supplication for all saints* (Ephesians 6:14 – 18)

First notice that we are told not to flee but to **stand**. The believer should flee when the flesh demands to be satisfied (*flee also youthful lusts*), but when in conflict with spiritual forces we are not to turn our backs (for there is no armor to protect the back), but to stand. In other words, we must confront the enemy.

In so doing we must *put on the armor,* and that means be clothed with the following:

Girt about with truth, we must live transparent lives of honestly and integrity and; *Casting down imaginations, and every high thing that exalts itself against the knowledge of God, bring into captivity every thought to the obedience of Christ* (2 Corinthians 10:5).

Then we must wear the *breastplate of righteousness,* having both a behavior that is righteous and an assurance that we are clothed with the righteousness of Christ (Romans 3:21, 22).

We must have our *feet shod with the preparation of the Gospel of peace* (Ephesians 6:15) – that is, we must *be ready always to give an answer to every man that asketh you a reason of the hope that is in you, with meekness and fear* (1 Peter 3:15).

Above all, we are told to take *the shield of faith.* In other words, we rest in absolute confidence in the promises of God and expect Him to work on our behalf.

Finally, we are to take the *helmet of salvation and the sword of the Spirit*, which we are told *is the Word of God. The helmet* is that which can protect our minds and it means having an assurance that you belong to Christ.

The sword of the Spirit is the weapon Christ himself used against Satan when tempted in the wilderness. To each temptation Christ responded, *It is written,* and then quoted Scripture.

Being able to employ the *sword of the Spirit*, implies you have hidden the Word of God in your heart. To take this weapon means to engage your mind with the Word by reading it, studying it in order to understand it, and memorizing it.

And we are to *pray always.* God is never far away and ready to help us. *Let us therefore come boldly unto the throne of grace, that we may obtain mercy, and find grace to help in time of need* (Hebrews 4:16). Thus supplied, we are ready for the battle.

Chapter Thirteen

STEP THREE:
RESISTING THE ENEMY

We have been discussing our relationship to God through Christ, and the provision of both defensive and offensive weaponry which God has made available to us as we face the battle. Now we move on from the training ground to the battle itself.

In this battle, we are told more than once that we must "resist" the devil. James writes, *Submit yourselves therefore to God. Resist the devil, and he will flee from you* (James 4:7).

Peter gives the same exhortation, *Be sober, be vigilant; because your adversary the devil, as a roaring lion, walketh about, seeking whom he may devour: Whom resist stedfast in the faith, knowing that the same afflictions are accomplished in your brethren that are in the world* (1 Peter 6:8, 9).

If those words conjure up pictures of a fearsome struggle, they should, because that is exactly what they are meant to do. Yet they also promise victory if we listen carefully to what they say.

James begins by saying, *submit yourselves to God.* There can be no victory apart from submission. If you are in rebellion against the will of God, if you are stubbornly refusing to obey the voice of the Holy Spirit, you will not have the spiritual strength to resist the devil.

The first thing we need to do is be sure there is no un-confessed and un-repented sin in our lives. If there is, we are *giving place to the devil.* In other words, we are giving him a foothold from which to attack and subdue us.

So, let's begin with honestly facing where we are in this matter. Thank God for His promise, *If we confess our sin, He is faithful and just to forgive us our sins, and to cleanse us from all unrighteousness* (1 John 1:9).

Once we are submitting to God, we will begin to see clearly.

We have already seen how Satan attacks through the mind. When a person writes, "sometimes it was as if a voice spoke to me and even told me in detail how to take my life"—guess whose voice he was hearing!

In fact, over and over again, in the final stages that lead to suicide, those who have recovered, those who have been resuscitated, those who have been spared, tell us that it was as if a voice was speaking to them and telling them to do it.

This is that *roaring lion* that Peter is speaking about, and he is fearsome indeed in battle.

What does the battle look like? Well, invariably as we have seen, there are factors that have led the person to a place of despondency or despair. These can be factors of stress, failure, personal loss, loss of a family member or a close friend, feelings of rejection, prolonged or terminal illness, and a host of other things, all intended to bring the person to a place of emotional instability and mental despair.

Now before even going on from there, look at that list again for a moment. What is there that is so terrible that it cannot fall within the scope of, *all things work together for good to them who love God, to them who are the called according to His purpose* (Romans 8:28).

Please understand, I am not trivializing those difficult things, nor have I lost sight of the fact that this promise is only to the child of God – that is the point I tried to make when we talked about your relationship to God. If you are not a child of God, I have no more answer for you than do the psychologists, and the "experts."

But if you are a child of God, then facing those difficulties you know that you have a God who has already proven His love for you in giving the best heaven had for your redemption. Take His promise and say with the Apostle, *<u>And we know</u> that all things work together for good to them who love God, to them who are the called according to His purpose* (Romans 8:28).

Tell God you do trust His wisdom in your life. He does know best for your circumstances, your abilities, your appearance, your health and everything else.

Remember how the eighth chapter of Romans ends, *Oh, the depth of the riches both of the wisdom and knowledge of God! how unsearchable are his judgments, and his ways past finding out* (Romans 11:33).

So the first defense is to take the Word of God and affirm God's good purposes in your life. If you do that, it will end the depression right there and you will have taken the first step to victory.

Let me suggest next that you memorize the following Scripture:

> *Now the God of hope fill you with all joy and peace in believing, that ye may abound in hope, through the power of the Holy Ghost* (Romans 15:13).
>
> *For I know the thoughts that I think toward you saith the LORD, thoughts of peace, and not of evil, to give you an expected end* (Jeremiah 29:11).

Believe God and let God be God in your life.

What shall I do if thoughts of suicide do come to my mind?

The first important thing is that you recognize the source of those thoughts. Satan comes with the purpose of destroying you. His chief goals are *to steal to kill and to destroy.* Once you understand that and you accept the fact that the impulse to suicide is from him, then you can fight.

Remember what Edershiem wrote, "The demonized were incapable of separating their own consciousness and ideas from the influence of the demon, their own identity being merged, and to that extent lost, in that of their tormentors."[59]

That is Satan's strategy. If Satan can keep you confused, and not aware that the thoughts that are tormenting you come from him, you will be immobilized and unable to fight. So, understand clearly the source of the temptation.

Now begin to take your ground and stand. Tell Satan (out loud) that you recognize him and what he is trying to do.

Tell Satan that when he tempts you, he is trespassing on private property, you are the property of God. Remind him that you belong to the King of Kings and the Lord of Lords

– the One to whom Satan himself will one day bend his unwilling knee.

> *Wherefore God also hath highly exalted him, and given him a name which is above every name: That at the name of Jesus every knee should bow, of things in heaven, and things in earth, and things under the earth; And that every tongue should confess that Jesus Christ is Lord, to the glory of God the Father* (Philippians 2:9 – 11).

Remind him that God has delivered you from his (Satan's) kingdom and placed you in the kingdom of God's dear Son, and remind him that you are purchased by the very blood of Christ. Yes! Remind him of the blood. Satan has no answer for the blood.

Now command Satan upon the authority of Christ to leave you alone. Will he obey? Listen to the testimony of the seventy that Jesus had sent out, *And the seventy returned again with joy, saying, Lord, even the devils (demons) are subject unto us through thy name* (Luke 10:17).

And when they reported to Jesus, He told them, *Behold, I give unto you power to tread on serpents and scorpions, and over all the power of the enemy: and nothing shall by any means hurt you* (Luke 10:19).

The last book of the Bible sums it up like this, *And they overcame him by the blood of the Lamb, and by the word of their testimony; and they loved not their lives unto the death* (Revelation 12:11).

Victory over Satan is your heritage as a blood bought child of God. Claim it and you will always have victory over the enemy.

But I believe those who are suffering from a temptation to suicide need to do one more thing. We have noted again and again, that this temptation is a focus on self. Charles Solomon called it, "The ultimate in self-rejection; and the epitome of self-centeredness."

What a seeming contradiction, yet it gets to the very root of the problem. When you are toying with suicide, you are consumed with yourself.

So let me challenge you to go another direction, get a different focus, and step out of your ego and turn your energies toward helping others. A visit to the ward of any children's hospital or old folks home should get you started. Is your situation really worse than theirs?

You may have to force your will to obey, but get busy and bless someone for Jesus' sake. Go on a missions trip, or help someone nearby, but get your focus on Jesus and on those around you and your self focus will begin to fade.

Find out how you can help. Ask God to give you a **servant's heart.** Make that one unique contribution that only you can make.

I really hope you heard that last statement. The God who designed and created you made you unique and there is one task that only you can do, one need that only you can meet and one calling only you can fulfill. Make that one unique contribution that only you can make.

Ask God to show you what you can do to bless someone who needs to be blessed. Offer to help someone this very day.

Share your testimony with someone who needs Christ. God will use you in ways you cannot imagine if you will only let Him direct your paths (Proverbs 3:5, 6)

For none of us liveth to himself and no man dieth to himself. For whether we live, we live unto the Lord, and whether we die, we die unto the Lord: whether we live therefore, or die, we are the Lord's (Romans 14:7, 8).

Once the enemy is exposed and the triumph of the Savior is understood and internalized, the path to victory for the believer is clear. *You shall know the Truth and the Truth shall make you free* (John 8:32).

That is the purpose of this book. In it – Suicide has been Unmasked! See it for what it is and set your will to utterly and finally reject it. <u>Suicide must NEVER be an option</u>.

Chapter Fourteen

FAITHFUL SAYINGS

The Apostle Paul used the phrase, *"This is a faithful saying, and worthy of all acceptance. . ."* in a number of places in his Epistles. What did he mean?

A "Faithful Saying," was a truth usually well known and accepted by the Church at large. It became categorized as a *Faithful Saying* by being repeated over and over and by being used in the early catechism (method of teaching by questions and answers).

Faithful sayings were catechistic phrases employed by the early church to teach sound doctrine and correct thinking. In a word, they were easily remembered clichés that one could hold on to in a moment of temptation.

One of the most familiar is part of Paul's testimony to Timothy, "*This is a faithful saying, and worthy of all acceptation, that Christ Jesus came into the world to save sinners; of whom I am chief* "(1 Timothy 1:15).

What I want to do is give you a number of Faithful Sayings, some found in Scripture and some outside of Scripture that, if you commit to memory, will keep you from *great transgression* (Psalm 19:13).

- Suicide is the ultimate in self-rejection; it is the epitome of self-centeredness.

- Suicide is a permanent response to a temporary problem.

- The greatest deterrent there is against suicide is the fear of God.

- Why not make a list of your reasons for suicide so you'll have them ready to give to God on the Judgment Day?

- There are no terminal cases with God.

- Suicide doesn't turn off the set -- it only changes the channel.

- Eternity is real and the only thing suicide ends is your opportunity to change your destination.

- The game of life has no winners and no losers until the last buzzer has sounded.

- Loneliness, despair, and failure are God on the phone calling you to come quickly into His presence.

- As long as there is God, there is hope.

- You can die unsaved, but you cannot die unloved.

- Climb out of your ego and make that one unique contribution that only you can make.

SCRIPTURE: READ, MEMORIZE, AND KNOW

The Scriptures have much to say about the way we think and what we think. Here are some Scriptures that can be your sword in battle with the dark powers of despair.

Keep thy heart with all diligence; for out of it are the issues of life (Proverbs 4:23).

Let the words of my mouth and the meditations of my heart, be acceptable in Thy sight, Oh, LORD, my strength and my redeemer (Psalm 19:14).

God has not given us the spirit of fear; but of power and of love, and of a sound mind (2 Timothy 1:7).

For I know the thoughts that I think toward you, saith the LORD, thoughts of peace, and not of evil, to give you an expected end (Jeremiah 29:11).

Now the God of hope fill you with all joy and peace in believing, that ye may abound in hope, through the power of the Holy Ghost (Romans 15:13).

Be careful for nothing; but in every thing by prayer and supplication with thanksgiving let your requests be made known unto God. And the peace of God, which passeth all understanding, shall keep your hearts and minds through Christ Jesus (Philippians 4:6, 7).

According as his divine power hath given unto us all things that pertain unto life and godliness, through the knowledge of him that hath called us to glory and virtue (2 Peter 1:3).

Finally, my brethren, be strong in the Lord, and in the power of his might. Put on the whole armour of God, that ye may be able to stand against the wiles of the devil (Ephesians 6:10, 11).

Submit yourselves therefore to God. Resist the devil, and he will flee from you (James 4:7).

For none of us liveth to himself, and no man dieth to himself. For whether we live, we live unto the Lord; and whether we die, we die unto the Lord: whether we live therefore, or die, we are the Lord's (Romans 14:7-8).

And it is appointed unto men once to die, but after this the judgment (Hebrews 9:27).

For I am persuaded, that neither death, nor life, nor angels, nor principalities, nor powers, nor things present, nor things to come, Nor height, nor depth, nor any other creature, shall be able to separate us from the love of God, which is in Christ Jesus our Lord (Romans 8:38, 39).

Finally, brethren, whatsoever things are true, whatsoever things are honest, whatsoever things are just, whatsoever things are pure, whatsoever things are lovely, whatsoever things are of good report; if there be any virtue, and if there be any praise, think on these things. Those things, which ye have both learned, and received, and heard, and seen in me, do: and the God of peace shall be with you (Philippians 4:8, 9).

Thou shalt not kill (Exodus 20:13).

GOD HAS SPOKEN
READ, MEMORIZE, AND KNOW

FOOTNOTES

1. World Health Organization
   http://www.who.int/gho/mental_health/suicide

2. Ibid.

3. Ibid.

4. Youth Suicide Statistics – Parent Resource Program; Jasonfoundation.com/prp/facts/youth-suicide-statistics/

5. http://www.nbcnews.com/health/health-news/ military- -n580276

6. Professional Development Guide; Department of the Air Force; 36-2241 (July 2007) pp. 420

7. http://www.militarytimes.com/story/veterans/86788332/

8. Solomon, Charles R. *The Ins and Outs of Rejection*: Heritage House Publications, 1976

9. Psychology of Counseling (1960) Clyde M. Narramore, published by Narramore Foundation.

10. World Health Organization
    http://www.who.int/gho/mental_health/suicide

11. National Child Safety Council – Dexter Gardner
    http://www.worldcat.org/title/national-child-safety-council-presents-this-is-dexter-gardner-signing-off/oclc/20348145

12. National Federation for Decency (NFD) Journal (January, 1986) page 13

13. John W. Ayers, PhD, MA
http://jamanetwork.com/journals/jamainternalmedicine/article-abstract/2646773

14. https://www.washingtonpost.com/news/to-your-health/wp/2017/07/31/internet-searches-on-suicide-went-up-after-13-reasons-why/?utm_term=.8908fe57f649

15. U.S. News & World Report; Gunn High School
http://www.usnews.com/education/best-high-schools/

16. The Atlantic; The Silicon Valley Suicides; Jamie Chung (December 2015 issue).

17. www.barnesandnoble.com/w/how-to-raise-an-adult-julie-lythcott-haims/1120327547

18. Blackburn, Bill, What You Should Know About Suicide, Texas, Word Books, 1982.

19. SOUNDING BOARD; Rational Suicide and the Right to Die — Reality and Myth; Yeates Conwell, M.D., and Eric D. Caine, M.D.; New England Journal of Medicine 1991.

20. *Psychological Medicine 40(5),* Bullying victimization in youths and mental health problems: 'Much ado about nothing'? pp. 717–729.

21. Ibid.

22. http://abcnews.go.com/2020/TheLaw/school-bullying-epidemic-turning- deadly/story?id=11880841

23. Bullying: (Dinkes, Kemp, & Baum, 2009)

24. Web: Change.org; Bullying

25. https://www.cdc.gov/lgbthealth/youth.htm

26. The New Atlantis; Journal of Technology & Society, Special Report – Sexuality and Gender (2016), Johns Hopkins University LAWRENCE S. MAYER, M.B., M.S., PH.D.; Paul R. McHugh, M.D

27. https://en.wikipedia.org/wiki/**Jim Jones**

28. Compton's Encyclopedia; Suicide, (1985).

29. http://www.nbcnews.com/health/health-news/military-suicides-most-attempts-come-soldiers-ever-see-combat-n580276

30. The Atlantic; The Silicon Valley Suicides; Jamie Chung (December 2015 issue).

31. Ibid.

32. Ibid.

33. Merrell, Gueldner, Ross & Isava, 2008; cited by The Atlantic; The Silicon Valley Suicides; Jamie Chung (December 2015 issue).

34. Vreeman & Carroll, 2007; cited by The Atlantic; The Silicon Valley Suicides; Jamie Chung (December 2015 issue).

35. The Atlantic; The Silicon Valley Suicides; Jamie Chung (December 2015 issue).

36. Ibid.

37. Angels & Demons; WWBI; Doctrine II; STEP III pp. 16

38. Christian Enquirer, Satanism "Thriving in North America" Volume 15, no.6/11

39. http://www.wnd.com/2012/12/satan-worship-motivated-sandy-hook-killer/

40. Ibid.

41. Ibid.

42. Ibid.

43. Ibid.

44. Ibid.

45. Ibid.

46. John Gill's Exposition of the Entire bible (E-Sword)

47. Edersheim, Alford; Life & Times of Jesus the Messiah; Hendrickson Publishers; pp.608

48. http://www.clebemcclary.com

49. Solomon, Charles R. *The Ins and Outs of Rejection*: Heritage House Publications, 1976.

50. Smith, Alford B.; Hymn Histories (1981); Heritage Music Distributors, Inc. pp. 232

51. Ibid. pp. 168

52. Professional Development Guide; Department of the Air Force; 36-2241 (July 2007)   pp. 421

53. Ibid. pp. 422

54. Ibid. pp. 422

55. Ibid. pp. 422

56. Wesley, Charles; Oh, For A Thousand Tongues To Sing.

57. (*Frontiers in Psychology*, Marc D. Hauser, Charles Yang, Robert Berwick, Richard C. Lewontin In cooperation with the Massachusetts Institute of Technology May 2014).

58. Professional Development Guide; Department of the Air Force; 36-2241 (July 2007) pp. 424

59. Edersheim, Alford; Life & Times of Jesus the Messiah; Hendrickson Publishers; pp. 608.

BY THE SAME AUTHOR:

The Prophetic Destiny of Israel & The Islamic Nations could hardly be more timely. How is the present conflict going to end? What will happen to Israel? -- To Islam? This book finds the biblical answers to those questions and more.

Amazed by Grace, the book that tells of God's marvelous faithfulness and miraculous acts in the life and ministry of Dr. Bill & Ruby Shade, is available in bookstores and on Amazon now.

Order your copy at:

BillShade.org

> Honestly, I believe this is the most important book I have ever written.
>
> Dr. Bill Shade

Dispensationalism in a Postmodern World is a fresh approach to a great subject. Whether you are a new student to Dispensationalism, or have been a life-long proponent, there is something here for everyone. Dispensationalism in a Postmodern World lays the necessary foundation by defining its terms, covers thoroughly and with great clarity the features of each of the seven Dispensational periods, and then addresses both the historic and theological challenges to the system. The underlying thesis of the book is that there is nothing this postmodern generation needs more than a metanarrative they can believe in and nothing provides that metanarrative better than Dispensational Theology. The Book is complete with a full color Dispensational Chart from Eternity to Eternity.

Order your copy at:
BillShade.org

Made in the USA
Columbia, SC
06 March 2018